WE REMEMBER

STORIES OF SEPTEMBER 11, 2001 VICTIMS WRITTEN BY FAMILIES

EDITOR
MAUREEN CRETHAN SANTORA
COVER ILLUSTRATOR
MAUREEN CRETHAN SANTORA

WE
REMEMBER

WE
REMEMBER

STORIES OF SEPTEMBER 11, 2001
VICTIMS WRITTEN BY FAMILIES

MAUREEN CRETHAN SANTORA

To order additional copies of this book, contact:
Xlibris Corporation
1-888-795-4274
www.Xlibris.com
Orders@Xlibris.com
44053

Contents

DEDICATION

This book is dedicated to all the victims who died on September 11, 2001. In addition to the 2,750 people who died in Manhattan, 184 individuals died at the Pentagon in Washington D.C., and 40 victims died in Shanksville, Pennsylvania. May we never forget them and may we hold their memories in our hearts forever.

Foreword

"Wake up Maureen! A plane has gone into one of the Twin Towers!" my husband said on the morning of September 11, 2001. It was my first official day of retirement from school. I had been an early childhood teacher for over 25 years and had retired as a staff developer on July 1, 2001. I jumped out of bed and went to our living room window. Our window faced Manhattan and we could see the Twin Towers every day. As I watched the heavy, black smoke pour out of the tower that was closest to us (Tower 1), I thought about how this could have happened. These towers were so enormous. They could be seen from every vantage point in the five Boroughs of New York City. As I watched I began to see another plane. It circled the second tower and in an instant, the second tower was hit. I knew then that this was not an accident.

The rest is history. We, in America will never be the same. The world will never be the same! In our world, we now have individuals who are filled with hatred and have vowed to harm all in the "western" world. On that day, 2,750 individuals in lower Manhattan lost their lives. These people were not in the military. They were not marching for any cause. They were not political activists demonstrating for a cause. They were simply ordinary folks who were going to work to support their families. The rescue workers were simply doing their jobs. They were trying to save lives. They died on that hate-filled day.

We, their families, will never be the same. Our lives as we knew it disappeared on September 11, 2001. Most of us are still trying to make sense of how this happened and why it happened. Our loved ones deserved better. This is the reason for this book.

Close to eight years later, we, the family members, are still grieving. We are still tying to make some sense of what happened to our world. We want people to learn about our dear children and brothers and sisters. We want students to understand that they were once young. They had the same dreams and aspirations. They loved to play sports. They sometimes had trouble in school. They had parents who loved them unconditionally. They had brothers and sisters who took care of them and played with them and had fun with them. Few of us who lost people on September 11, 2001 were able to say "good-bye", or "I love you", or "I'll miss you forever". We are still grieving the losses we experienced. We want everyone who reads this book to understand how special our loved ones were. Writing stories of remembrances will help all to understand and learn things about the people who we loved so dearly. We want everyone to know that those who died were once young and grew up to become wonderful adults.

When I first thought about writing stories about September 11, 2001, I believed that we needed to help younger students learn about the day. My first two books, *The Day the Towers Fell* and *My Son Christopher,* are children's picture books. As I researched, I learned that there were no books written for either middle school or elementary school students. As an educator for many years, I felt an obligation to provide information that would help students remember what happened on that hate-filled day. I wanted students to learn about some of the victims who had died. I wanted students to be able to identify with the victims in regard to the similarities they may have with the process of growing up. I wanted students to understand clearly that much more than two famous towers were destroyed; lives were shattered. Not only did people die, but families were emotionally torn apart by this terrible tragedy. I want everyone who reads this book to learn about what hatred did to all of us. The world will never be the same.

I began to spread the word. I contacted the 9/11 family organizations that I knew and wrote a letter explaining my expectations and hopes for this special project. All of the writers who submitted stories personally lost someone they loved very much. All wrote from their hearts. All expressed to me that it was very difficult to write about someone they loved who was now not with them. Still to their credit, they wrote their stories. I have read each and every story. I cried at times. I laughed at times. I was touched emotionally by every tale. Adding the pictures seemed to be the natural thing to do. It provided a face to the story. I have learned about these special people who were just going to work on that dreadful day. I feel I know them a little.

As you read about the victims, I hope that you can identify with many of their traits and characteristics. I hope you realize that growing up is sometimes hard, but if we have dreams we grow up to be successful and helpful and knowledgeable and most importantly, we have a wonderful life.

Finally, it is my hope that all who read this book realize that life can be short. It is not how long you live but how you live your life that matters. A wise person (my daughter Kathleen) once said to me, "Don't sweat the small stuff". Life should be joyous at times. Life can be hard at times. Make the most of each and every day. Most importantly, tell the people you love that you love them every day. These should be the lessons of September 11, 2001.

I am so honored to be among the wonderful families that were a part of this special project. May those that died on September 11, 2001 never be forgotten. May we think about them often and may they be in our hearts.

My heartfelt thanks to Xlibris Publishing Company and all my friends and my family who read, re-read, and helped to make things as "perfect" as this book could be. A special thanks to my daughter Kathleen and my husband Al who were the final proof readers. They were not only 2 of the writers but they honored my dear son Christopher by making sure that the stories were as "perfect" as they could be. In addition, I must thank my husband Al who put up with my frustration at times and was understanding about the importance of this project. "A good man is hard to find" as they say. I have a great man.

As with my other two books, all the profits from the sale of this book will be going to a special charity. The Christopher Santora Educational Scholarship Fund (*www.christophersantora.com*) was selected for the first two books that I wrote. For the *We Remember* books, a special fund to help the rescue workers who are now so terribly ill has been selected. Helping those who worked so hard and tirelessly to help all of us seemed the natural and right thing to do. None of the authors will benefit financially from the sale of this book. This is our legacy for our children, brothers, and sisters.

Maureen Santora
Editor

Thomas Patrick Holohan Jr.

By Iris Holohan,
Thomas' mother

Whenever I see the name Thomas Patrick Holohan Jr. my heart swells with love for a boy, a man, my rock, my son! To those who never met him, I will give you a glimpse of who he was and answer questions such as "Did he enjoy sports?" "Did he excel in school?" "What were his interests?"

As I look back, I remember a cute little boy with fantastic dimples. Dimples that lit up his face whenever he smiled. Thomas, or as the family called him, "Chip", was a quiet child but not shy. He was the second oldest of five children, and was the only boy in the family for the eleven years before his brother was born. His quote to his father when told that he had a little brother was, "You wouldn't be kidding me Dad?" Don't forget Chip already had three sisters: Mary-Alice, Jennifer, and Megan. That was quite a burden for a young boy.

Some people let you know they are in a room by their loud laughter or noisy demeanor. Chip was definitely not that type. Even at a young age he seemed comfortable with who he was and was accepting of others, which made him a good friend.

School was viewed as a necessity that all children had to do. There was seldom any great enthusiasm about waking early to go to school. He just accepted it throughout his grade school years. By the time Chip was in fourth grade, he decided that it wasn't necessary for his parents to oversee his homework anymore. He felt it was his work. Seems he took responsibility for himself early in life.

Chip with his brothers and sisters
(Chip 4th from left)

Graduation—Baruch
College in NYC

Chip at 32

As with most of the children in Little Neck, Chip truly enjoyed riding his bike. He and his friends would often ride almost a mile to fish in Little Neck Bay. Chip used his determination and his bike to deliver newspapers in the neighborhood for years, encountering some interesting situations along the way. While working his route one day, he came across a homeowner holding onto a roof gutter after a ladder had slipped out from under him. Chip to the rescue! A few months later he came home late from his paper route. No explanation was given until I insisted on one. As he told it, "An old lady fell while carrying home her groceries. I had to help her home and then went back for the groceries." A thank you note arrived in the mail a few days later from the woman expressing her thanks. Chip told us, "It was no big deal" but I knew better.

By the time he was twelve his smile was enhanced with shiny stainless steel braces. Braces are never fun, but they are necessary. As it turned out they even worked to his advantage one day in junior high school. An altercation arose with another student after school. The other, older guy walked away with cut up knuckles after coming into contact with Chips' braces.

The years spent at St Mary's High School were busy ones, between the heavy school work load, school sports (swimming and track), and working after school a couple days a week. His friends in school now called him Tom. The light in his room was on until early morning hours at times, as he worked on a school project that was left to the last minute to complete.

During those times he still found time to be a big brother. I remember the day Chip took Sean, his brother, to the Bronx Zoo. Chip was about eighteen years old and Sean was six.

As the story goes, they were in line for the elephant ride when one of the elephants became agitated after a young child ran up to the elephant and startled it. The animal reared up and bellowed, frightening the people around. Chip then told how everything worked out fine because the line became so much shorter for him and his little brother. I was not happy!

Going to college seemed a natural progression of schooling for Chip. He hadn't decided exactly what course of study he would pursue, but it definitely would involve taking courses in math. It was a subject he did not find difficult. He attended Queens College for one year and then transferred to Baruch College in Manhattan. Finally, he decided to major in finance. The day he graduated with his BA in finance was a wonderful day for him. He worked so hard and rarely complained. The ceremony was held in Madison Square Garden. The sun seemed to shine everywhere that day.

Chip worked as a bank auditor in an international bank in the Wall Street area of Manhattan for three years. A few years before, he had applied to the FDNY. There are always thousands of applicants for the job of firefighter in New York City and the competition is high for the job. After taking both the written and physical exams, you sometimes have to wait a long while to be called. Chip scored near 100 on both parts, and when the envelope arrived for him to report for training, he was thrilled. "What about your college education?" I asked. He responded, "I'll use it in the Fire Department and work my way up in rank."

Being married to Colleen and having three children he loved filled up a great deal of his life. He coached young Tommy's football team, took his daughter

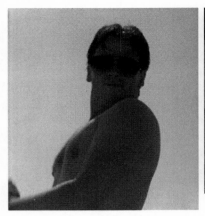

At Jones Beach

Chip with 1st son, Thomas Patrick III

Firefighter Thomas Holohon
(June 2001)

At the Long Island game park

Caitlyn (who he called his princess) to preschool, and played with baby Liam. Even with all that, Chip always found time for his sisters, brother, and I when we needed him. And we did need him. He was our rock!

Tommy (as his fellow fighters now called him) was assigned to Engine 6 in lower Manhattan, and was studying for the Lieutenant exam. He never got to take it. On September 11, 2001 he died in the North Tower of the World Trade Center.

We all remember the words he frequently expressed: "There's an easy way or the right way, which way are we going to do it?" He lived his life the right way.

Kevin Dennis

By Patricia Bingley,
Kevin's mother

Kevin was born in London, England on July 13th 1958 weighing 8lbs 15 oz. As a baby he was very healthy. He was also very energetic, never still, and when he started to find his voice, he never stopped chatting in his baby talk. One of the things I remember well about him as a baby was how he always wanted me to wipe his chin when it got wet through his dribbling. Even from that age he was quite fussy.

I was always finding shops that sold smart boys clothes. My last spare penny went on buying him unusual outfits, and during his young years even he became interested in looking smart himself. In fact, he was a pleasure to dress.

At the age of 3, he never stopped asking questions. It got to the stage where he even questioned why he could not go to school. Where we lived there was a small private school quite near us and I enrolled him, mornings only, for 13 *guineas (British money)* a term. I vividly remember the first morning I took him; he walked into the school like he had been going there all his life, and as with all his schooling, he loved it.

As a family, when we could afford it, we went for 2 weeks every year to a Butlins Holiday Camp. They were family camps that were great for children. One year I entered him into The Smartest Boy Competition and he won. First prize was a train set. After that he wanted to enter into every competition.

7 months   With his Gran, me, and my brother

Smartest Boy competition, 1st prize: train set   In his Gran's garden playing
Cowboy and Indian

With his Grandmother at
Butlins Holiday Camp

Kevin always had a dog as a little boy and teenager. I can see him now—walking with the dog pulling on his coat, brushing it off and carrying on walking. I remember the day his father took us for a drive to the seaside. We had a boxer dog named Chummy who was very excitable, and Kevin wanted to take him with us. My husband got some pills from the veterinarian to help quiet Chummy for the journey, but because he timed it wrong the dog did not become drowsy until we arrived at our destination. Kevin was in pain laughing because his father had to literally carry Chummy half the day. He also had a goldfish which he nearly lost because one sunny day he decided that the goldfish needed some sun, so he put the fish in the garden and it nearly fried. Kevin was very upset when that happened.

One of his hobbies as a little boy was making airplanes. I bought the box sets of different types of balsa wood and he would make the planes and hang them from the ceiling of his bedroom. Over the years he also collected Boys Annuals (magazine for boys), which he read from cover to cover. Kevin was a treat to buy things for because he looked after everything he had. In fact, when he grew up, I gave a lot of his books to a nephew and they were nearly as new as when they were bought for him.

In England when Kevin was at school there was a scholarship that children had to sit for when they reached the age of 11. It was called the "11 plus." They were at primary school when they sat for it. Kevin was mad about airplanes at that age, and wanted to become a pilot. In order to achieve that ambition, he wanted to eventually go to an aviation college called Cranwell. But to get there, you had to pass your "11 plus" and also have a relative who had been or was an officer.

Kevin was a very studious young boy and had always received good reports from school. He wanted his father to write to Churches College to get him an interview there because the boys there went into the forces as officers. At that time he had not even sat for the "11 plus" but he was confident that he would pass and wanted to make sure that they would accept him. I remember he was going abroad with his school for the first time just after he took the exam and his words to me before he went were, "Mum I know a letter will be waiting for me when I get home to say I have passed." And there was. Right from a little boy, Kevin was always so sure of where he was going, and that sometimes surprised me.

Of course he passed his "11 plus" and got an interview for Churches College, which he was also invited into. So during the six week holiday I was running around getting all the things he had to have, including a trunk to put everything in, and having name tags ordered, as Churches College was a boarding school for boys. He was so excited and not a bit bothered about leaving home, and again when we traveled to Petersfield with him and his trunk, he walked into the college like an "old boy." I was sad that he was going away from home but I did not dare show it. He made 4 great friends during his time there, and one of them was his best man when he married in New York in 1987. I think being an only child it was very good for him to live with other boys, and of course the discipline helped him for the future. He loved Churches College and I used to go visit every Wednesday and take him and his little friends out to the village teashop for tea and cakes.

Kevin's teenage years were spent at the College, and during the holidays he was with me and my second husband in the Public House that we ran in London (a London Beer Pub). From the age of eleven through his teens he often flew out to Australia to be with his father, who had moved there when we divorced.

Kevin's father had a friend who worked for the only foreign exchange in Sydney and during a holiday in Australia, Kevin went to the exchange and decided from then that he no longer wanted to be a pilot, but wanted to get into the money market. So, when he left the college he went into the city of London and got a junior position in The Bank of America, and became very successful as a money dealer. When he was 21 he was what they called "head hunted" by a bank in Manhattan. Although I was again sad that he wanted to leave England, I did not show it. I just said that I wanted whatever he wanted, and if he thought he could have a better life in the States and be as successful as he was in London, I thought he should go for it. In the city they used to call him, "A young man in a hurry."

Although Kevin was all those miles away, he was on the phone at least twice a week, and within three months he sent for me and my husband to go over there for a three week holiday. He had a lovely little apartment uptown and he seemed so happy with his life and was getting on well at the bank. He took us all over Manhattan in his car and you would have thought he had lived there all of his life. I remember him taking us to Washington for the day. When we arrived he drove into this underground car park, and this black lad came up to him to park his car and when he heard Kevin's English accent, his eyes rolled as he said, "Man are you from Beetle Country?" and we laughed.

Kevin was so good to us during our visits to the States when he was single, and every time we flew out he always lived in a different part of Manhattan—uptown, midtown, and downtown, and he soon knew the city like the back of his hand. Kevin made a lot of friends and was very successful. I always said he was my cockney boy living the American Dream. Although he lived all those miles away from me, we were still very close and he spent hours on the phone telling me what he was doing as well as asking about my life too. He would also ring me up when England Football was on TV, as he was a great fan of the game, and would ask me to put the phone by the TV so that he could listen to some of the game. He also took me to Yankee Stadium to see the Yankees play. In fact, he loved to watch a lot of sports. His father was a big Rugby player although they only played Rugby at the college. Kevin never liked playing; he always said it was too rough for him.

Kevin was the best son a mother could have. Thank goodness he was very successful in his career and lived a wonderful, rich life. He always wanted me to fly over to share some of it with him, but I was scared of flying so I never went as often as he wanted me to. I used to say to him, "As long as you are happy and healthy, I am happy just being at home and listening to you on the phone telling me about your lovely life."

He was the light of my life and that light went out on the 11th of September, 2001, and as the years go by it does not get any better but you handle it better. I will think of him every day until I die and I miss him so very much.

Primary School Photo,
8 years old

Age 11, arriving at
Churches College to begin
life at boarding school

Taken in Carnway Street,
Swinging London in 1968

At Heathrow airport
leaving for America

With me at holiday
home in Long Island

Taken at Woodstock in
America. He loved his hats!

With me in
Manhattan, 1987

With his Christmas presents, age 34.

Age 30, Uptown Manhattan

This photo was in New York Times
beginning of last year

Dennis Michael Mulligan

By Patricia Mulligan,
Dennis' sister

Dennis Michael Mulligan was born on May 6, 1969, the fifth child of six children born to his mom Marie, and dad Ed. He had two sisters and three brothers. One of his sisters, Theresa, died shortly after she was born in 1963, and so he never got to meet her, but he always asked our Mom about her. He knew he had another sister.

Dennis was a funny boy as a child. He liked to play video games and would dance around and twist his right leg in the funniest ways when he played those video games in restaurants where you had to stand in front of the controls. That was in the "old" days. Now kids sit in front of their own televisions with their own controls.

Dennis spent the first six years of his life living on University Avenue in the Bronx on the fourth floor of a five story walk-up apartment building. That means there was no elevator. When he was six, we moved to a place called Throgs Neck, also in the Bronx, and bought a house on a street called Indian Trail. It was called a trail because it was a walking path; only two people could walk side by side down this trail, which winded its way along the East River. Did I mention that our house was literally on the water, just twenty yards from the river? It also faced the Whitestone Bridge and the Throgs Neck Bridge to our left. At night, we always looked at a pretty skyline with bright lights; it was like Christmas time all year!

As a young boy (approximately 6 yrs old), fishing with his dad, Ed Mulligan and his brothers (behind the camera), Kevin and Brian Mulligan. What a catch!

Posing with his brothers, Kevin (left) and Brian (center). Dennis is in white sweater, approximately 7 yrs. Old.

Posing for his High School Graduation photo—St. Raymond's High School for Boys in the Bronx, New York.

On vacation, playing in the pool with his brother Kevin. Dennis is on top! Approximately 10 yrs old.

At his graduation from the NYC Fire Academy with his proud mother (1994)

Cruise a few years after becoming a firefighter

We could also see the Manhattan skyline right there in front of our house each day when we stepped outside. It was just behind the Whitestone Bridge. It was beautiful. (The Whitestone Bridge would take people from the Bronx to Queens, just in case you were wondering.)

Did I mention how smart Dennis was? When Dennis was growing up, he always studied hard at school. He often spoke about what he wanted to be when he grew up. He wanted to be a doctor—a pediatrician. Dennis loved people. He loved helping people. As Dennis grew, his entire family was excited that he wanted to be a doctor. All families love that, right? But as Dennis grew older, something changed. He started talking instead of becoming a fireman. It seemed that he had switched what he was passionate about. You know what your passion is, right? It is that thing that you *know* you really want to do. You want to be a veterinarian. You want to be a doctor. You want to be a pilot or an astronaut. We all know that you can be ANYTHING that you choose to be. Dennis decided that he wanted to be a fireman. I think he decided this when he was older. Dennis was in his late teens, maybe twenty years old, when he knew he wanted to be a fireman. The thing is, when you decide you want to be a fireman or policeman, you have to first take a test. You just can't apply for the job. You have to take a written test, a physical test, and a psychological test. This means that the City of New York wants to make sure that you can do a good job for New Yorkers. So, Dennis took two tests: the Police test and the test to become a fireman. He was first called to be a policeman. Now, Dennis didn't really want to be a policeman. He wanted to be a firefighter. But, he decided that if he became a policeman first, then maybe he could become a firefighter sooner. So, Dennis became a policeman. It was so funny seeing him in a police officer's uniform! He was our brother, not a policeman! We had a big party for him when he graduated from the Police Academy, and we have some great pictures. At that time, Dennis' older brother Michael was already a policeman. In fact, he may have already been promoted to the rank of Sergeant. So, Michael had some fun making fun of the rookie cop—his brother!

Dennis was good at anything he did. He was a good cop, but he was only a police officer for a short time because in less than a year, the Fire Department of New York (the FDNY) called him to become a firefighter. He was never happier. We did not have another party because we just had one less than a year earlier, but we were still happy for our brother.

Dennis joined the New York City Fire Department in 1994. He was so proud of himself and so were we. You've heard about the FDNY being referred to as a brotherhood; now Dennis didn't have three brothers, he had thousands! And, do you know what? It's true. Firefighters treat each other like family. They look out for each other. They take care of each other. Maybe that's why Dennis loved being a firefighter.

NYC ('99)

Standing and holding milk. He was about to make himself a White Russian (cocktail) and pretended to give the milk to his neice, Kaitlyn Mulligan, held by his father, Kevin Mulligan. Seated on the left is Dennis' brother, Brian Mulligan (1998).

At a friend's wedding

Dennis' family celebrating his brother Michael's 40th birthday
Kneeling in front: Dennis Mulligan
Top row, left to right:
Brian Mulligan (brother),
Patricia Mulligan (sister),
Kevin Mulligan (brother),
and Edward Mulligan (father)

Dennis was a firefighter for over seven years. He loved what he did. His family didn't know it, but he had earned several medals of valor during his career as a firefighter. That means that he risked his life to save others on several occasions. Although firefighters risk their lives every single time they respond to a call for help, on some occasions, Dennis was really brave and his

Dennis in front leading the way down the steps with 2 other members of his company (#2 helmet) and another firefighter.

Mulligan Memorial Foundation—softball tournament attended by hundreds of Dennis' friends and family each year—the foundation raises money for educational scholarship for High School Alma Mater, St. Raymond's High School for boys in the Bronx. Also, scholarships are offered to firefighters and their children. From left to right, Kevin Mulligan (brother), Michael Mulligan (brother), Patricia Mulligan (sister), Dierche Mulligan (sister-in-law), Brian Mulligan (brother), Edward Mulligan (father)

bravery helped others. The funny thing is that we, his family, didn't know about his acts of bravery until after he was killed while evacuating the North Tower of the World Trade Center. We didn't know this because he didn't tell us. He didn't save others because he wanted his family or the world to think he was a hero. He saved others because he simply wanted to help people, just like he dreamed he could when he wanted to be a pediatrician. Guess what? He saved more people as a firefighter!

Mayor Giuliani described the rescue efforts of the firefighters and police and other rescue workers as the greatest rescue mission in the history of our country. The swift response of hundreds of firefighters as well as police and other rescue workers resulted in thousands of people being safely evacuated from the World Trade Center before it collapsed. Thousands! How many pediatricians can say that they saved thousands of lives?

On the morning of September 11, 2001, Dennis was coming off duty at Ladder 2 on 51st Street in Manhattan. He was heading to the Jersey Shore where he owned a home with several of his firefighter buddies. It was a beautiful September morning. At 8:46 a.m., a plane, American Airlines Flight 11, struck Tower 1, the North Tower of the World Trade Center. The North Tower was 110 stories high. It, along with the South Tower, or Tower 2, was the tallest building in Manhattan. The plane struck the building between the 93rd and 99th floors. The plane hit the building pretty high. A lot of people were killed when this happened. The estimates are that approximately 1,360 people died at or above the 93rd floor. That's a lot of people. I didn't get to talk to my brother that day, but I believe that made him very sad and very mad. He didn't have to work that day. He could have went to New Jersey and lain on the beach, but he didn't. Instead, my brother, Firefighter Dennis Michael Mulligan, hopped on the fire truck and rode extra. That means that he was not needed or, at least, not scheduled to work on the morning of September 11, 2001. He worked because he wanted to help.

Dennis and nine of his fellow firefighters, which included a Chief and a Captain, responded to the World Trade Center the morning of 9/11. We know that immediately prior to the building's collapse, Dennis was seen evacuating the lobby of the North Tower. I am told that he wore his typical "mugsy smile"—that was his nickname and he was always smiling! I am also told that he was afraid. They all were: firefighters, police officers, and civilians. It was scary. The buildings were on fire. Two planes had struck the buildings, the North and South Towers. People were killed. Some people were jumping from the buildings because the fire was too hot. Dennis stayed.

At approximately 10:29 a.m., on 9/11, the North Tower collapsed. Our brother, my parents' son, was killed. Dennis was 32 years old. He was not married. He did not have children. He was our brother. He was my parents' son.

Dennis would say, "Circle the wagons," and "feed off your strength." That is what we have done. I, we, did not think we could survive without him. He was incredible. Our love for him was endless. He was our brother, our son. We live in his memory. His love sustains us.

Until we meet again, **Our** brother, **Our** son. We love you.

George Cain

By Rosemary Cain,
George's mother

The story began on May 13, 1966. It was a beautiful spring morning, which also happened to be a Friday. That was OK with me—I have no superstitions, and throughout his life I would tell him he was my "lucky charm." He was also born three days before my birthday, so he was my birthday present as well. He was number three in the Cain family, joining his older sister Nancy and his brother Dan. Two years later he would become older brother to baby sister Erin, a position he held throughout his life. He loved his family, and in his own quiet way, carved his space in the dynamics of his siblings.

Certain events stand out in my mind in the younger years of George growing up, and one very important one was when he was about 10 years old. We always spent weeks of summer vacation upstate New York at my Aunts house in the Catskills. It's a big old house with lots of nooks and crannies, literally. There were always a bunch of kids running in and out, doing various things and having a great time as kids should in the summer. We, my aunts and I, were always big on antiques. One day we planned a trip to a town about an hour away. Off we went, leaving the kids in the care of their fathers and older siblings. We were about a mile out of town and I was driving when my Aunt said, "Is that you Georgie?"

Sure enough, I looked in my rear mirror, and there he was, by himself, walking along the country road in his own little world and happy, I am sure, with what was in his mind and heart.

At that time, little did I know that the signs were there; the little boy wandering along on that country road had the spirit of the man he grew into. George became adventurous and loved the outdoors. He grew up tall and strong.

While in high school, he became an avid skier; he loved the sport and it became a large part of his adult life. After graduating high school, he worked with a carpenter and learned many skills. He eventually went out west, lived in Colorado and earned his living building log homes, always finding time to ski. He had taken the test for the New York City Fire Department and knew he had to wait a few years on the list, so in the meantime he lived a great life working as a carpenter. When the snow started to fall he would hit the slopes.

Eventually, the Fire Department called and he came back home. We were all so happy for him, especially me because I knew he would have the security of a wonderful job, health benefits, and retirement. These were things that George never gave too much thought to. He reconnected with old friends and life picked up where it left off.

The hours of the Fire Department gave him lots of free time, time when his friends were working, so he picked up another hobby—golf. Like everything he did, George wasn't happy until he became good at it, and he had the patience to keep at it until he was a good golfer. George also loved music. He and his high school buddies attended many concerts and he was always listening to music. He had a tremendous CD collection and lots of concert shirts. He was a big Gerry Garcia fan and I have heard many funny concert stories from his friends. It was always a great time with lots of laughs—happy memories for all of them.

George had a wonderful attitude about life. The Fire Department afforded him the lifestyle he loved. He was always true to his heart. He didn't plan on marriage anytime in the near future; that would have interfered with skiing and golfing. He loved to take off on a minute's notice and go biking or hiking through the woods. He ran the New York City Marathon, climbed Pikes Peak and lived his life to the fullest, all while being a firefighter. He always had his tent handy and loved to camp out under the stars. I remember one summer he drove around with a canoe on top of his truck.

His greatest role in life was being an uncle. Uncle George was the best uncle a kid could have: Christmas parties in the firehouse, Fourth of July, fireworks in the city, camping at Montauk, and best of all, learning to ski. He taught his nephew Chris and niece Meaghan to ski. His godson Conor never had the chance to ski with his beloved uncle, but in the years since, he has taken off and now snowboards. I am sure Uncle George is so proud of all of them because they are living his legacy.

George lived a life full of love, kindness, courage, and selflessness. George knew the dangers of the Fire Department, but despite all of the danger, there is a tremendous spirit of goodness. The camaraderie of the job and working with others who have the same spirit brings a wonderful fulfillment. The spirit of all who perished on September 11th will never die because of the strong legacy each of them left. The world is a better place for them having been here. I thank God every day for the gift he gave me on May 13, 1966.

My Brother Firefighter George Cain

By Nancy Nee, sister

Losing my brother, FDNY Firefighter George Cain on September 11th, is an event that has changed my life, my world, and the life of my family, my children, and my other siblings. But thankfully, we have wonderful memories of him and his life. George had a life many people envied, for he had such a good outlook on life and made the most of everyday. He shared his life with us, and we shared ours with him, so there are no regrets for us. He made every effort to be a part of all of our lives and the lives of my children. I'm so thankful that he was their uncle and that they have great memories of him. I am honored to call him my brother. But I always felt that way, long before September 11th.

I am the oldest of four kids, each of us being two years apart. Georgie was number three and was four years younger than me. We were two boys and two girls. I always felt closeness to him, something that not all people can say they have. It was unexplained, unplanned, just there, a connection. It lasted our lifetime. I suppose that happens in life. We instantly feel a connection to one sibling over the others, or one coworker over another. Or someone you meet at a party or business function. We automatically tune into one particular person, over all the others in the room and we can't explain it, it just is.

That's the way it was for Georgie and I. Very easy. It was never something I felt I needed to work at with him. Being with him was sheer pleasure and fun. He exuded a passion for life and the people he cared about. He was passionate about just about everything he did in his life. Whether it was skiing, golfing, riding his bike, or just hanging out with friends and family, he enjoyed himself to no end.

Maybe being the third child, and second boy, made him realize he needed to establish his place in the family. He needed to make his place and create his legacy, even as a kid. He loved to laugh, at the expense of others or himself. It didn't matter, as long as he was laughing. As a kid, he was on the small side and kind of walked on his toes, something he finally outgrew around the age of fourteen, but I think it was something we were all concerned about for his sake. Would he always be small and have a funny walk? Thankfully, no! He started to grow and gave up the tiptoeing. He finally reached 6'1" and was more fit and athletic than anyone I know. And he finally surpassed his friends in height.

His nickname at the firehouse was "Dude". His laidback demeanor earned him that name, but he could just as easily have been called "the jokester" for his sense of humor and love of practical jokes. From the early days of our childhood, he loved to tease our younger sister Erin by hiding her stuffed animals under the couch cushions and lying on top of them, and then he would watch her freak out! His sense of humor was always with him. Upstate one summer, my Uncle

Jack asked him to run outside, in the rain, to see if his cigarettes were on the picnic table. Georgie ran out in the rain, saw the cigarettes lying there, and ran back inside to tell my uncle, "Yeah, they're out there!" He didn't bring them in with him. He just told my Uncle that they were out there, left outside to get drenched in the rain.

When my daughter Meaghan was around seven or so, Georgie teased her into licking a battery, and she did it, because her uncle told her to. If you've ever done this, (and who hasn't) you know what she tasted, and she was not happy with him. She wouldn't talk to him for the rest of the day. She was really mad at him, but it didn't matter, she loved him anyway!

He also had a mischievous side to him, not bad, just a daredevil kind of spirit, like nothing bad would happen to him. Another time upstate, he took a cousin's bike and rode down a very steep mountain road, alone. I think he took out someone's fence at the end of the road! Thankfully he wasn't hurt, just a little banged up. It was the same kind of daring spirit that took him to Colorado on his own, where the daring behavior continued. He bungee jumped, parachuted and heli-skied, where you jump from a helicopter onto a mountain and ski down. He liked to do things with a group or on his own. He could hike or go golfing by himself and still have as good a time as if he was with a group of friends.

The comfort of being on his own and wandering off brings up another memory of another time upstate. My mom and my aunt used to love to go to auctions and they dragged all of us kids with them. There were usually at least 6-8 kids at any given time. They would buy all this stuff and then try to get it and all of us back in the car. We'd be sitting with all of this stuff all over our laps, cramping our heads and what-not. So this one time, we all got in the car, drove back to my aunts house, unloaded all of this valuable stuff or "antiques", as they liked to call it. A while later, a woman called the house to ask if we were looking for a little boy named George, who was back at the auction house. Yes, he got left behind! Not only did he get left behind; no one even realized it until the phone call. And, there were no cell phones back then! We still laugh at that story.

As a mother of my own three teenagers now, two boys and a girl, I love to hear them talking and laughing with one another. It makes me happy to know that they are bonding now, to form the relationships of a lifetime. And things are not always rosy, so don't get me wrong. They fight plenty, which is totally normal. But I feel it is so important to teach them to treat each other with respect and appreciation, to respect each other's feelings and privacy, to be considerate of each other's lives and attitudes. I sometimes wish I could go back to my own childhood with the maturity and knowledge that I have now, and be given another chance to perhaps be a better sister to my own brothers and sister. This is the one time

Additional Information from Your Utility

Delivery and System Charges	Charges for owning, operating and maintaining the electric system, and for certain on-island generation. Also includes certain transition charges of $0.013518/ kWh collected on behalf of the Utility Debt Securitization Authority.
Basic Service	Fixed daily charges for connection to the electric system.
KWH	Kilowatt-hour. Electrical energy consumed if 1,000 watts are used for one hour.
Power Supply Charges	Charges for costs associated with the purchase of fuel (e.g. oil and gas) used to produce electricity and for the purchase of power.
Revenue-Based PILOTs	(Payments In Lieu Of Taxes) State and local taxes on utility revenues. This does not include property taxes assessed on the electric system, which make up 15% of your bill.
Efficiency & Renewables Charge	Provides for the costs of PSEG Long Island's energy efficiency and renewables programs for our customers.
NY State Assessment	Assessment imposed on all utilities and collected on behalf of the State.
Suffolk Property Tax Adjustment	The amount collected from Suffolk County customers representing the overpayment of property taxes to the Shoreham taxing jurisdictions from a court-ordered legal settlement dated January 11, 2000.
Meter Multiplier	Converts recorded use to total use on meters that are designed to only record partial use.
Sales Tax	State and/or local sales taxes.

Payments are accepted at any customer office or authorized payment location.

Payments may be mailed to: PSEG Long Island, PO Box 888, Hicksville, NY 11802-0888.

Please write your Customer ID on the face of your check or Money Order and make payable to PSEG Long Island.

PSEG LONG ISLAND

we get to establish that foundation for the rest of our lives. I recently came across a saying, that I truly believe sums up the sibling relationship. It goes like this:

> When you lose a parent you lose part of your past.
> When you lose a child, you lose part of your future.
> When you lose a sibling, you lose both.

In loving memory of you George, forever your sister!

XO Nancy

Stephen P. Russell

By Cliff and Marie Russell,
Stephen's parents

Stephen P. Russell entered this world on May 19, 1961—a beautiful, healthy 7 lb. 5 oz boy. He was the youngest in the family and had two older brothers. All three boys grew up in a very loving family environment. This story will only be about Stephen.

Until he was 18 months old we lived next door to his grandparents. At this time we moved into a home we purchased together with his aunt and uncle a few blocks from the original home. This home was on the water and helped to shape the kind of life he led. We will get back to that later.

Stephen attended St Rose of Lima Elementary School in Rockaway Beach, NY, graduating in 1975. He then attended Beach Channel High School and graduated in 1979. In high school he became interested in music and learned to play the trumpet and the cornet. Although he was always a friendly type of person, music seemed to make him more outgoing. He belonged to the orchestra and the jazz band. He went to work summers during his last two years as a first mate on a yacht going out of Lawrence Yacht Club in Lawrence, NY to Essex, CT plying the waters of Long Island Sound. In the early 1980's he attended Kingsborough Community College, graduating with an Associate in Liberal Arts Degree. While in college he worked nights and weekends at Pergament Home

Center in the paint department. He stayed at this job after graduation, full time, and eventually became manager of the paint department.

In the mid 1980's he decided it was time to move on. He took classes to become a securities investment counselor. He passed the test and received a series six license, which enabled him to obtain employment with a securities firm and work as an account executive. While there he decided that his in/out desk sorter didn't hold the papers needed for the job. He came home and designed and built a desk sorter that did the job for him. A few days later he was making more of them. It seemed that everyone in the office wanted one. We thought this was very funny. He worked at the securities firm for a few years but decided that it was not the type of work he wanted to do for the rest of his life.

Taking the test for the FDNY was in the back of his mind but of course, one had to wait until the test would be announced. He was also always interested in woodworking and had made some things for himself. He took a job with a firm that manufactured custom-made furniture. There he learned design and also how to use laminates. He joined the Carpenter's Union and then went to jobs as they opened. During his tenure as a carpenter he also went into the building and maintenance of cooling towers for private and commercial office buildings in Manhattan and New Jersey. It was this well-rounded background that gave him an unusual combination of skills in the field of woodworking, plumbing, and electricity.

Stephen took the FDNY test and passed both the written and physical. He continued working at his job on the cooling towers while waiting for the Fire Department to call him. However, two weeks before he was to be called he slipped and fell two stories into a cooling tower he was working on. He broke his wrist and a vertebra in his back. The FDNY gave him until the next class in Jan.1994 to get into shape. He worked with a physical therapist in order to be able to pass the training at the FDNY Academy. He worked hard, persevered, and made it. Graduation from the Academy was in March 1994.

He served as a firefighter with Engine Co.55 and was looking forward to taking tests to climb the ranks of the Fire Department when he died on Sept. 11, 2001.

While at the firehouse he put his carpenter's skills to work. From what we've been told he was always working around the firehouse. He would be building, fixing something, anything to keep busy. When it came to fixing things, if he didn't have the tool to do the job he would invent one. He built an activity cabinet, a huge Maltese Cross which had the pictures of everyone who worked at the house in the year 2000, and a memorial cabinet which can be seen as soon as you walk into the firehouse. Little did he know that his picture and those that were lost with him on 9/11 would be the first to be placed into this cabinet.

Steve lived in an apartment in our home so we saw him just about every day. We will each try to tell you about some of our most poignant memories.

This is mom speaking about you, Steve, our youngest:

You hated it when I introduced you as the "baby" of the family. I remember the gold fish you won at the church bazaar and left in a glass of water overnight. You woke me up crying because it was dead in the morning. We ended up buying an aquarium and filling it with goldfish.

We saved some ducklings from the bay and took care of them. I arrived home from work and immediately knew something was wrong from the look on your face. One duckling had died. You had it waked on a paper towel on the kitchen counter. We gave it a proper burial.

About 15 minutes after you left for work one day you phoned me. You found an injured swan on the North Channel Bridge and put it behind a barrier so a car wouldn't hit it. You asked me to please call the NPS at the bird sanctuary to

Half way through the construction of the hydroplane

Steve, "cruising" in his hydroplane named "Black & Blue" because of the black and blue marks you end up with after a ride.

DISPLAY CABINET DESIGNED AND BUILT BY
FF STEPHEN RUSSELL ENG.55

come and get it. I called but we never heard anymore about it. You showed this compassion all your life—from helping a neighbor that had fallen to concern for dad and I and your brothers and their families. This compassion for all living things followed you into adulthood and into your life's work as a firefighter.

You were very thoughtful, even at an early age. You were ten years old when on Easter you presented dad and me with two plants about 4 inches high. I can still see your large eyes looking up at us. You were so proud that you bought us a gift by yourself. One plant didn't make it, but the other one is still thriving (31 years later) and is now three plants that reach the ceiling. There are two in our apartment and one in your apartment. We still go up and water it once a week. You were my shopping partner. You knew just the right gift for everyone.

You started me on the computer and taught me the basics. I still play solitaire nights that I can't sleep.

I miss hearing your car pull into the yard, your knock at the door, sitting down for dinner and bringing Rhonda in to eat when she's with you. You're at our table in spirit every night. You knew that I walked on the boardwalk every day. On days that you would go jogging you would take me with you. I would walk a mile while you jogged three miles and we would meet at your car.

I went to art class twice a week and also had an easel set up at home. You made sure that you would be available to show up every time we had an exhibit or an art auction. I'm sure it must have been very boring for you.

Steve's father has asked me to write his thoughts and memories.
These are some memories from your father:

I saw you as a truly straight arrow. You were never any trouble. You would always watch me as I would be doing some chore or repair around the house—willing to learn how to do it yourself. I taught you how to row—feather the oars—remember?

I taught you how to sail at an early age—first in the sailing dinghy and then in our sloop. By the time you were eleven you had mastered the art of sailing.

Because of where we lived, it was only natural for you to be interested in all water sports. The first thing you did was build your own hydroplane. When you were old enough to go to work you saved enough money to buy your own boat for water skiing. After that came the wave.

You took scuba diving lessons and eventually became a dive master. You went all over on dive trips proudly displaying your under-sea artifacts when you arrived home. You taught your older brother and nephew how to scuba dive. This led your nephew to go to college and obtain a degree in oceanography.

This same nephew and his brother were so inspired by your life as a firefighter that they took the test for the FDNY, passed and intend to enter the Fire Department as soon as they are called. You were always doing something with me around the house to keep it in repair. You would be upset if I did anything without your help. I have to admit that there were times when you had some ideas that I hadn't thought of.

When you first moved into your apartment you decided to build your own bedroom set. It was quite a task but you ended up with a custom made set that is great. We'll never be able to get it out without taking it apart so it will have to stay there. We'll use your apartment for guests.

When you would arrive home after a snowfall we would hear the shovel scraping against the sidewalk in your effort to clear the snow away before we could get to it.

We had planned to do the two back porches together, but of course that didn't happen. It has taken us this long to finally find someone to do them over. So far we have the estimate and we're waiting for the work to begin. I would have been happier with you on the job.

*   *   *

It is extremely difficult to write about a son that meant so much not only to his parents but also to his brothers, their wives, and his nephews, niece, and long-time girlfriend. He was the most thoughtful, compassionate, sensitive person that we've ever known. He had a smile and a glint in his eye that immediately drew you to him. He was the son that any parent would be proud of, the son you dreamed you would have—the one that anyone would want for a son. His handsome, smiling face said it all. One person wrote us after his death that he had a kindness and simplicity that made him stand out from all the rest. A truer statement has never been made.

*   *   *

Steve,

You'll never get older in our memories. No matter what, we will always remember you as the young, handsome, athletic, thoughtful person you grew up to be. You are missed, never forgotten and loved forever and ever.

Love always, Mom and Dad

PS—Steve, We had to purchase a new VCR because you weren't around to reset the time after an electrical outage. We bought one that sets itself.

*   *   *

Poem about my uncle Steve who died in the World Trade Center

" . . . I sat for long hours knowing that I probably wouldn't find out till next dawn."

By Erika Russell, age 13

You were my favorite buddy; you were always there.
Sometimes you seemed to be the only one who cared.
Visiting Grandpa and Grandma's house was always fun,
'cause I knew you would be there,
cleaning your boat in the sun.
Then one day it happened,
All I could think about was you and my dad;
The airplanes bombed into the towers
And you were the first two I though of and I got very sad.
Thinking that you wouldn't make it,
But knowing you were strong,
I sat there for long hours that day,
I probably wouldn't find out till next dawn.
My dad was the strongest when he got the news,
It was his brother and he looked somehow confused.
Like he knew what had happened and wasn't yet sure
whether to smile because we found out,
or to cry because you were gone.
My brothers Christopher and Cliff probably got hurt the worst;
They loved him so much yet they had to let him go.
I cried for days but seemed to move on,
Because I know you're in a better place,
Still that brave fireman who has always been strong.

This Poem was written in a car while we were driving to the city on some 9/11 meeting. On 9/11, we had full view of the towers burning at the sky, except for the clouds of black smoke, were cloudless. A clear blue sky always makes me think of seeing those "black clouds."

Merci Russell

Dearest Steve

Awaking to a sky clear and blue
Especially then, we have thoughts of you
We desperately search the azure sky
Hoping to see a cloud roll by

Then thoughts of you run through our core
Your voice
Your laugh
Your smile
Your eyes
Calling your name
Your knock at the door
Little things that meant so much before

We remember the day with the cloudless sky
When we suddenly saw black clouds go by
We could feel our hearts pound
As the building came down

While dad watched through his scope
For some possible sign of hope
I ran upstairs to ask in prayer
Your life to spare

Could we possibly dare
To hope you were not there?
Hope waned, and we cried and give a sigh
The day we watched you die.

                                    By Marie Russell

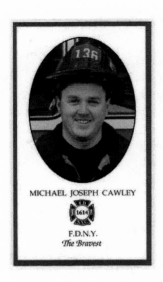

MICHAEL JOSEPH CAWLEY

F.D.N.Y.
The Bravest

Michael Cawley

By Margaret and Jack Cawley,
Michael's parents
The Perseverance of a 13 year old

Michael had 16 first cousins. Three attended Archbishop Molloy High School ahead of him. One of his cousins, Brian Mulqueen, always took Michael to all the sport activities, which led Michael to only want to attend Molloy. Michael was a very good student in grammar and was even invited to take a special exam for Regis High School, a prestigious scholarship school in Manhattan. Michael told us, "Why would I want to take the test for Regis when I am going to go to Molloy? I want to put it down as my first, second, and third choice."

Michael took the Catholic Co-op test and thought he did well, but when the letter came he had not been accepted to Molloy. Obviously he did something wrong on the exam. We were totally devastated, knowing how Michael wanted to attend this school. I called his principal only to be told that she had other very good students who were not accepted into their second choices and Michael had two other good schools to choose from. I called his previous principal who suggested Michael write a letter to Brother John Klein, the president of Molloy. Later that day Michael fell while playing basketball and came in with an obvious broken wrist. I taped it to a spaghetti box, but before Michael would go the ER he had to write his letter to Brother John Klein. Apologizing for his poor penmanship

Michael 7th or 8th grade wishes

Michael 7 yrs old,
first communion

Michael 3 years with newborn sister Kristin

Michael 6th grade

August 2001 Michael, Dad,
and brother Brendan in a Hampton pub

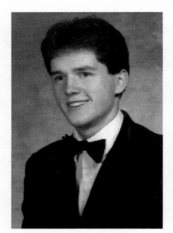

Michael 1987, Graduation
from Molloy High School

Michael and Brendan Confirmation Day, 1986

due to a broken wrist, Michael poured his heart out about his love for Molloy and asked for consideration.

Within the next few days, Michael's cousins descended upon Molloy to plead Michael's case but were told that nothing could be done, as more applicants were accepted into Molloy than there were seats.

One day in April when our kids had a half day off from school, Michael came down the stairs with his Easter blazer and slacks on and said, "Mom will you take me to Molloy? I want to see Brother John Klein." I said okay and when we arrived at the main office, Michael announced to the secretary that he wanted to speak with the principal and gave her his name. Brother John Klein came out and Michael towered over him, a lanky 6 foot 13 year old. Brother John Klein said he usually did not meet with students under these circumstances but had remembered Michael's letter and his cousin's visit. We sat in Brother John Klein's office and he reviewed Michael's seventh grade marks and stated Michael should have made Molloy with his excellent grades, but again, there was no room.

Michael said he would attend another school for a year and then come to Molloy. Again Brother John Klein said there was no guarantee this could happen, and I was not in favor of this idea. Brother John Klein told Michael that he had 7 boys with similar situations as Michael's who were asking for consideration. He wanted to know why he should choose Michael if there was an opening. Michael answered, "Brother John Klein, I have been coming to Molloy already for the last 2 years with my cousin, I know every thing inside and out about Molloy and I belong here more than anybody."

Brother John Klein decided that Michael should register for his second choice school and that if nothing happened by a certain date, Michael should attend that school for the next four years. As the weeks went on Michael said to me, "Mom if it does not work out I will go to Holy Cross, but I don't want to see you crying anymore."

Certain things happen in a way that makes an imprint in your mind that you will never forget. Five days before the cut-off date, I was folding socks and it was late in the afternoon. The phone rang and it was Brother John Klein telling me a father of an incoming freshman had been transferred out of state and that he had chosen our Michael to fill the opening. I gave him our heartfelt thanks and told him he would never regret it. It seemed like ages before Michael came home and when he came upstairs, I of course began to cry tears of joy while telling Michael he was going to Molloy. He jumped down the stairs in a way that I thought he would go through the staircase window, and ran up the block to the convent, banging on the door to tell them he was going to Molloy. In the summer, Michael attended the incoming freshman camp and when he came home he told us, "I had the most awesome time of my life".

On the first day of high school, all 400 plus freshman are put in a race and guess who came in first place? Michael J. Cawley! He came home thrilled saying,

Michael's Legacy

I hope my achievements in life shall be these...

that I have fought for what was right and fair,

that I have risked for that which matters,

that I have given help to those who were in need,

and that I have left the earth a better place for what I've done and who I've been.

Michael in Disney World, Florida, 2000

Michael and Brendan

In Loving Memory of

MICHAEL JOSEPH CAWLEY

Born into life
April 6, 1969

To the Lord
September 11, 2001

New York City Firefighters

As most of us stopped, to see
the fire in the sky,
you were in the trucks, passing us by.
As the unthinkable horror,
makes us shed a tear,
you entered the building,
in your rescue gear.
As we sat in panic praying for no more,
you were climbing stairs floor by floor.
We sat confused, awed, and in strife,
you were looking, hoping, and
praying for life.
As the building came down,
we feared you would too.
But God gave you wings
and instead you flew.

-Emily Dickenson

MICHAEL JOSEPH CAWLEY

1614

F.D.N.Y.
The Bravest

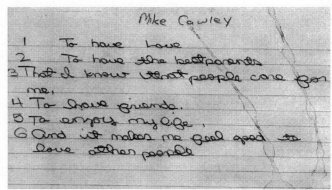

Mike Cawley

1 To have Love
2 To have the best parents
3 That I know that people care for me,
4 To have friends.
5 To enjoy my life,
6 And it makes me feel good to love other people

"Now I really feel I belong at Molloy." Michael won a medal in every race he ran for the first year but had to stop running after he developed stress fractures in both lower legs. He took this in stride and became the time keeper at the races.

Michael was in so many clubs, peer groups, and spiritual encounters that he was awarded the Marcellin Champagnat award for school spirit at graduation. He had spent four wonderful years loving Molloy each day. He made wonderful, caring friends that remained as a "rat pack" even through they all went off to different colleges. These friends became part of our extended family. At graduation, Brother John Klein spoke of the type of student that Molloy wanted, and then proceeded to read the letter Michael wrote as a 13 year old hoping to attend Molloy. While he did not mention Michael's name, there I was again, crying as usual with my other kids telling me to stop. When Michael was applying to colleges, Brother John Klein wrote a beautiful reference for Michael saying that Michael was the student he would most remember from the entire class because of his enthusiasm and service to Molloy.

When we had to put some plans together for Michael's Memorial Mass, our youngest son Brendan, also a graduate of Molloy, wrote Michael's obituary requesting any donations be forwarded to scholarships at Molloy in honor of Michael. Brother John Klein presented a beautiful and most moving homily about our beloved Michael at his mass. As we prepare for Michael's 7th Memorial Foundation Benefit we now have 12 yearly scholarships for fireman children attending Molloy.

Michael was also a counselor at the Marist Brothers summer camp for children with both physical and psychological challenges in Esopus, New York. Throughout his four years at Molloy, he and his "rat pack" friend would go up and work as counselors for a few weeks, then come home and return again. Michael's Memorial Foundation also provides support each year for this camp, and they have a granite bench honoring Michael at the camp.

In 2002, Michael, along with several other graduates of Molloy who died on September 11, 2001, was admitted to Molloy's Hall of Fame.

In August of 2001, a few weeks before 9/11, our Michael had a barbeque to celebrate Dave, his best friend from Molloy, who had just completed a year of intensive therapy for a malignancy. All of his Molloy "rat pack" came to his home which he had bought just 6 months before. His dad and I kept telling Michael we wanted to buy him a barbeque grill for his backyard as a house gift, but Michael kept putting off buying it. I asked him what he was going to use for his barbecue, he gave me one of his favorite statements, "Mom it's no biggy." After Michael's death his Molloy friend Eric told me that when he called Michael the morning of the barbecue and asked Michael if there was anything he could bring, Michael said "How about a barbecue." that was our Michael who lived life with ease.

IT IS NOT THE YEARS IN YOUR LIFE,
BUT THE LIFE IN YOUR YEARS.

———

Linda George

By Carolyn George,
Linda's Mother

Linda was born in 1974, the youngest of three children. She had an older brother and sister. She was a content baby and a happy child. Linda was very content to play by herself and as she grew, she played school continuously with her stuffed animals. She had them all in a circle and was always bossing them around.

Her brother Bryan teased her a lot, but was very protective of her. Her sister Diane was her playmate and they were always putting on shows and skits for us.

Linda liked school and was a very good student. She was a born leader even in elementary school, and had many friends who frequented our home.

Linda was very organized, and as a ten year old kept score for me when I coached her sister in softball. Her room was her domain and she kept it very tidy.

In junior high Linda excelled academically and in sports. She played basketball, soccer, and track. She was her class leader and always was defending the underdog. Linda was always taking on a cause. She became friends with a girl in 7th grade who was very insecure and lacking in confidence. Linda took her under her wing and even took her on her first trip away from home. They became lifelong friends and she knew that Linda was always there for her. Years later Linda became her bridesmaid.

Linda loved to talk on the phone

Linda George, 10, daughter of
Doves Coach Carolyn George,
keeps warm and keeps score.

High School valedictorian

High School friends at home

Linda's high school friends

While in junior high Linda took over a baby sitting job from her sister, and became an important part of the family. They had four young children and traveled a lot. Linda traveled with them and was lucky enough to spend two weeks in Hawaii. Linda learned a lot—especially honesty, loyalty, and responsibility.

Linda left junior high with an athletic award. It was decided that Linda would join her sister at a private Catholic high school. She was very unhappy for the first week, crying at night that her life was ruined. Her sister, being a senior, was not much help.

Linda tried out for the soccer team and made varsity. There she met life long friends and played alongside her sister. She loved her soccer coach and rallied the team together to buy the coach, who was pregnant, a stroller and presented it to her at their last game. Linda also was on the basketball team and helped them have a few winning seasons. We liked to call her "pigpen," because she was always on the ground, hustling and grabbing for the ball. In college she played rugby and found her niche on the ground getting covered in mud.

Linda was class treasurer and a tyrant when it came to collecting money and organizing the funds. She worked on many committees, fund raisers, and even helped paint the school gym. As a senior Linda was awarded the Telegram and Gazette Student Athlete award. She was also awarded the "Academically." She attained the highest grade point average and was selected as Valedictorian of the class of 1991.

Linda entered Providence College, where she met many friends. Because Linda was so neat, (her sister said she folded paper clips) we were concerned that she would have a roommate who was untidy. She met her match as Michelle was neater than Linda.

While in college Linda's sister gave birth to identical twin daughters. As a single Mom, Diane struggled. Linda was such a help to her and she adored the twins. Often she took them to her dorm room where all her roommates made a big fuss over them.

College was a wonderful experience for Linda. She worked hard and played hard. Work study was a big part and she was able to help pay her tuition. Linda graduated from Providence College with a Bachelor of Arts degree majoring in marketing.

After graduating Linda accepted a job with TJX Corporation. Within a year or two she was promoted to the title of buyer. Linda loved her job and enjoyed the travel involved. One of her most memorable trips was to Hong Kong.

While at TJX she met and fell in love with a fellow employee. They met at the company volleyball team where Linda was the manager and captain. Linda and Jeff became engaged and were to be married on October 20, 2001.

On Sunday, September 9th we had a bridal shower for Linda. Her Dad and I went back to her house after the shower and watched her open gifts again. She

Providence College, Rugby

College roommate, Michelle

Buffet concert

Classmates, Providence College

couldn't have been more excited. She was also excited because she was going on a business trip to L.A. the following week. That was to be the last time we saw her.

On September 11, 2001, Linda was on her way to Los Angeles with six other TJX employees. They were to open a new Marshalls Store and Linda was to assist in the buying of new merchandise.

Seven women from her company were on American Airlines Flight 11, which hit the first tower.

Our hearts were broken after Linda's death. There is nothing worse than the loss of a child. Our family has remained strong and we survive with the support of family and friends. Linda's spirit lives on in our hearts and we try by our example to bring some support to others who have experienced losses.

Memories of Laura

By Lorraine Ragonese,
Laura's mother

It was 1976 and I was sitting in the auditorium of John Jay High School in Brooklyn, New York where my sixteen year old daughter, Laura, was being inducted into the ARISTA Society for High Honor Students. I was so proud. After all I'd been through with her as a child, my Laura was here tonight standing up with the best of John Jay's academic students. But wait, there was more. Laura was also asked to sing at the ceremony. My daughter always had a beautiful voice and was not shy about performing (in fact, she was a bit of a ham.) Everyone at John Jay knew she loved to sing. It was a real honor for her to be asked. The only thing I didn't know was what song she had chosen to perform. When they introduced her, she stepped up to the microphone, and the music began to play. Suddenly, I felt my eyes fill with tears. The song she had chosen was *"You and Me Against the World."* This was a song that had very special meaning to both Laura and I. It's a song about a mother and daughter who are best friends. The daughter sings about how her mother always protected her, and how through out life, they were always there for each other. Let me tell you why this song has such meaning.

Laura was a child with developmental problems. She was born prematurely, small and frail, barely weighing six pounds. She had tiny pointed ears and the nurse in the delivery room said she looked like a "Pixie." From that moment on I called her my

44

Laura on vacation, Washington DC, 2000
(40 yrs old)

We Remember . . . Laura Marie
Ragonese-Snik, Sept. 11, 2001
Photo taken in 1998, 38 years old

To Maria,
      Look how beautiful I look! (HA-HA). Let's hope all our dreams come true and we'll always be friends (if not family!)

                                                              Love,
                                                   Your friend, Laura
                                            ☺ Smile! God loves you!

"Pixie Girl." Because of her low birth weight the doctor told me it was likely Laura would have some developmental problems during her early childhood. She might have some physical problems, trouble learning, or be slower to mature. With Laura, we saw a little bit of everything. She had very poor eyesight which needed thick

Laura (16) and Maria (13), center, 1976

Laura (19) and Maria (16), 1979

glasses to correct, and mentally and emotionally she was a year or so behind most kids her age. She didn't communicate well and was very within herself. Yet I knew, in only the way a mother can, that she was smart. I knew there were lots of thoughts and feelings inside her trying to come out. So I worked with her everyday. I sent her to mainstream school even though at times, it was so difficult for her to understand and follow the rules. I taught her right from wrong and made her responsible for her actions, and slowly but surely she started to comprehend the world around her. It wasn't always easy on her. Sometimes, I pushed hard. But one day, as if a light suddenly went on, she began to make progress. All our hard work had paid off.

Laura was the middle child of five. Mary Ellen and Michael were her older siblings, and after Laura, came her brothers, Frank and Larry. Each of them had their own special relationship with Laura. I asked them if they could share some memories of Laura with you because I really feel, through their eyes, you will best see what Laura was like as a child.

Brother Michael:

When I think of Laura as a child I always remember her zest and excitement whenever she got a gift. She loved the holidays, especially Christmas (she loved her birthday too). She'd get excited about these occasions weeks in advance as she wondered what surprises were in store for her.

Our parents always made Christmas very special for us. We all were instructed to go to bed early on Christmas Eve so that we could give Santa time to arrive with our presents. Then at midnight my Dad would ring his special bell and that would signify that Santa had come and gone, and that "The Ragonese Christmas" has officially begun.

One Christmas stands out in my mind because it is the perfect example of how Laura's child-like excitement made our lives so rich, full, and comical. Well

46

Laura, far left, 9 years old, 1969

Laura (left), 7 yrs old, 1967

left to right
Michael, Frankie,
Mary Ellen, Larry, Laura

Laura (bottom-center) 4 yrs old, 1964

Laura (right), 5 yrs old

this one Christmas, my parents sent us all upstairs and we tried to keep ourselves busy. My brothers, Frank and Larry who were six and three, went to bed, but were not sleeping. My older sister, Mary Ellen and I were checking our lists hoping we would get the new albums and clothes we had wanted (she was thirteen and I was eleven so you know how important these things were to us.) And Laura, who was ten years old, was the most exited of all. She just loved the gift thing and it didn't matter what the gift was. Just getting something special—anything—was such a thrill for her. Ripping the paper and opening the boxes were also part of the fun . . . She could hardly contain her excitement

Anyway, we are all upstairs waiting for what seemed like days; just waiting for the bell to ring. My brothers started wrestling (a nightly occurrence) in their bunk beds, Mary Ellen was reading her Tiger Beat magazine, I started to watch some TV quietly, Laura was singing a song to herself (not so quietly). And then the bell rang . . .

Well, my sister, Laura was so excited and caught up in the moment that she forgot everyone and everything. She bolted down the stairs, literally knocking my little brothers out of the way, causing them to tumble down the rest of the stairs. My older sister and I just stopped and gasped as they rolled down the stairs. Laura stepped right over them, not even looking back, as she raced into the living room toward her gifts, leaving my brothers sobbing in her wake! I just cracked up laughing; it struck me as so funny.

Of course everyone was fine; Laura was scolded for not being considerate of younger siblings and me for laughing. But we had a great time opening those gifts and boy did Laura let that wrapping paper fly!!!

Sister Mary Ellen:

It was my sister Laura's first day of school. My brother Michael and I are older (not by much) so we were already in school. Mike and I were always very serious, and a bit scared, and we *always* followed the rules. Our sister, Laura, on the other hand was *always* herself, always such a free spirit and always marched to her very own drummer. That being said, she thought that she could just come and go as she pleased.

At some point, during the course of the morning, Laura decided she wanted to see me (she needed to tell me all about her teacher, her classroom, and how her day was going.) So, when the teacher wasn't looking, she just got up out of her chair and left her classroom to find me. I can still see her amazing smile and feel all of her excitement when she found me in my classroom. She just marched right into my room and started talking to me.

Of course, there are rules, but my teacher was very understanding and allowed me to escort Laura back to her classroom. I tried to explain to Laura that she needed to ask her teacher to leave the room, and that she had to stay in her own class, and I would see her after school ended for the day. She just gave me that sweet faced look of hers, kissed me, and did what I asked for the moment. Needless to say, Laura did that a few more times that day, including running off of her line, when my class passed hers in the hallway on the way to the bathrooms. Each time she just wanted to let me know how much she loved me, and to give me a big hug.

Our teachers made sure that my mom knew what had transpired that day. All my Mother had to do was to tell Laura if she didn't listen to her teacher and follow the rules, she would not be able to go to school anymore and be "big" like Michael and I. She told her she would have to stay at home with her and still be a baby. Well the next day, Laura followed all the rules because even at that young age, she loved school.

Even though Laura eventually learned the lesson of self control, there were still days, when our classes crossed in the hallway, I could tell that it took all of her will power not to run right over to me and give me a big hug!!

Brother Frank:

Growing up, we were all die-hard Yankee baseball fans. I remember so clearly, Laura teaching me how to pitch, and playing endless games of whiffel ball with me in the back yard—that backyard in Brooklyn where Laura was my playmate and my coach. She never got tired or frustrated. She could play with me for hours and make me feel like I was pitching at Yankee Stadium.

Brother Larry:

I was the baby of the family and sometimes it was Laura's job to watch me or keep me occupied. I always looked forward to those times. We didn't need toys or games to have fun because my sister, Laura, had a great imagination. We didn't have a record player or records until we were older but that didn't stop us. Laura would make these items out of paper and cut them out. They became real for us as we spun the paper records and sang our favorite songs.

As you can tell by her sibling's stories, Laura was slow to mature yet I never felt this was a negative. I felt it gave Laura a very special view of the world. She always saw the good in things and people. She always had deep faith in God. And music was always her expression. This was how Laura found her way in the world and became a successful person.

Laura had many ideas on what she wanted to do with her life. Her dream was always to go to college and become a teacher for handicapped kids. But when she graduated high school that dream got put on hold to marry a high school sweetheart. Two years later, she became a mother; something else she always wanted to be. I can honestly say that the day her son, James, was born was one of the happiest days of her life.

As you know, life doesn't always turn out as planned. Laura was divorced shortly after her son was born. This left her a single mom and she had to return to work full-time. She took a clerk typist job with a small insurance group called Frank B. Hall. She was quickly promoted to administrative assistant, client representative, and then on to a manager in the Special Risk Department. Laura had a way with people and the "gift of gab," so dealing with clients all day long was the perfect job for her. She also got the opportunity to travel a lot which she loved to do. As in her personal life, everyone in her professional world loved her too.

Her company was bought out several times over the years she worked with them, and in the early 90's became AON Consultants, and AON Consultants resided in the South Tower, on the 101st Floor, of the World Trade Center. Laura was thrilled. She was excited to be working in one of the tallest buildings in the world. With Laura, everything was a positive.

Not long after her move to the World Trade Center, Laura met a wonderful guy that believe it or not she met on a blind date. His name was John Snik. They dated for a year and were married soon after that. Finally, Laura found the man of her dreams. A month before they were to celebrate their 4th anniversary, tragedy struck.

You all know what happened on September 11, 2001. My sweet, kind and precious daughter did not survive the terrorist attacks on the World Trade Center. We were told from survivor accounts that Laura stayed behind to help her coworkers. We heard how she was calming and comforting friends that were scared even though, somewhere in her heart, she must have known she should be getting out of that building. Laura was a truly good person, and this was evident even in the last moments of her life.

In 41 years, Laura had come so far from that vulnerable little girl who depended on me for everything. She had accomplished so much, embraced every moment and was truly happy. I believe that my sweet girl had no regrets. She loved her life; her husband and her son. She loved her family. She was blessed with wonderful friends who adored her, and no matter what life brought her way; she tired to meet it with a smile on her face and a song in her heart.

Our family has learned to live with this tremendous loss and tragedy but the heartache never goes away. We try to remember how Laura lived, not how she died, and we let that inspire us. I hope it inspires you too.

Addendum:

Laura, whose story you just read, was my best friend. We met when I was 11 years old. Our families—the Ragoneses and the Bartolottas—have known each other since 1974 (34 years).

For as long as Laura lived, we were (what you girls would call today) "BFFs"—Best Friends Forever! And like any good BFFs, we always wished we were sisters. Well, we sort of got our wish years later when I married Laura's oldest brother, Michael, which made us sister in laws (that was good enough for us!!) But even before that we were always sisters of the heart—"soul sisters" was how we used to sign our cards and letters.

All of my memories of growing up with Laura include singing and dancing either in her garage or in my living room. When we first met, we formed a singing group with her brother Mike and my sister, Roe called: "THE AMERICAN REVOLUTION". We sang into our hairbrushes, sketched out photos of our costumes, and planned to take the world by storm someday. When the singing group didn't pan out we moved on to Broadway. We decided to put on our own production of the musical "Grease". So we got all our friends together, cast the roles, and rehearsed for weeks. Laura's parents were so supportive. They made the garage look like a theatre, putting a sheet up for a curtain, setting up chairs for family and friends, and serving refreshments. I will never forget Laura (who played the role of Marty) singing "Freddy, My Love" in baby doll pajamas and her hair in rollers. We had such fun!

Then disco came on the scene and the new dance was "The Hustle" which we mistakenly tried to learn in my living room on a day when my mom had just bought new lamps. She told us not to dance in the living room, and of course, we had every intention of obeying until we put all the dance steps we learned together, and just wanted to try it "once" with the music . . . And then, when Mike went to spin my sister, Roe, she crashed into me, I crashed into Laura and Laura crashed into the new lamp—Yikes!! Lucky for us, the lamp was able to be repaired. But needless to say, we were banned from my living room for weeks and my mother never stopped telling that story!

I don't know why it was fated for Laura to be in the Towers on the morning of September 11th. Sometimes, I still wish she would have been late for work or away on a business trip that day like so many others. But what I do know is that Laura was at her job, a job she *loved*, with people she *loved* working with. She *loved* New York City and *loved* working inside the Trade Center. She had many opportunities before September 2001 to accept other job offers elsewhere, but she wanted to be there. Working for AON Consultants gave her a great sense of pride, joy and accomplishment, and as much as it still breaks my heart, I know there is nowhere else she would have chosen to be. Laura was truly happy with her life and that gives me great comfort, especially on the days that are still so difficult without her.

I will leave you with something near and dear to my heart: Laura's motto. She wrote it on everything—notebooks, letters, pictures, cards—since she was 13 years old it goes like this with the smiley face drawing:

Smile, God Loves YOU!
I know this is what she'd want you to remember about her!

Maria Ragonese
Best friend and sister in law

Jonathan Lee Ielpi

By Anne Ielpi,
Jonathan's mother

During an interview by a TV reporter who was doing a story on our family after 9/11/01, my husband and I were asked when we knew our son, Jonathan, was going to be a firefighter. My husband, Lee, was quick to answer, "The day Jonathan was born."

Lee, Jonathan's father, was a New York City firefighter and also a volunteer firefighter in our hometown of Great Neck. Lee rose through the ranks up to Chief of the Great Neck Vigilant Engine and Hook and Ladder Company. When the fire whistle sounded, Jonathan, and our other son Brendan, would race out of the house to sit in the front seat of their father's chief car and sound the siren as they sped through town to a fire or emergency call. Most of the time, the boys were in the car before their father. When Jonathan eventually became the assistant chief of the same fire department, I saw the same excitement in his sons' eyes as they raced to calls with their dad.

Our yard was always busy with our four children, Anna Marie, Jonathan, Brendan, and Melissa, and a variety of other children from the neighborhood. After cutting down a huge maple tree in our backyard, Lee and a few friends built a playhouse on top of the old tree stump. Being a city firefighter and volunteer firefighter, Lee was able to bring home old turnout coats and helmets which the

Jonathan Lee Ielpi,
1 yr old

FDNY—Graduation with wife Yesenia
and son Andrew

Jonathan, Anna Marie, Melissa, and Brendan

2001 Great Neck, Memorial Day Parade
Brendan, Lee, Jonathan, and Austin

Local Volunteer
FD Parade. 09/09/01,
Jonathan and Austin

Camping with Andrew and Austin

Lying in bed with sons
Austin and Andrew

Rescuing his sister, Melissa from the
playhouse in backyard

Spring 2001

neighborhood boys used as they played firefighter. One day, Jonathan, Brendan, and their two friends boarded up the windows of the playhouse, and talked Melissa (their younger sister) into being a victim. They threw smoke bombs into the playhouse and waited. When the smoke started seeping through the windows and door and Melissa started screaming, they responded to the "fire" in full fire gear with the fire hose stretched, and rescued screaming Melissa from the burning inferno. It was a day the boys, Melissa, and I will never forget.

Jonathan's dream was to be a firefighter. In order to reach his dream, when he was twelve he joined the Alert Junior Firefighters, where he rose to the rank of Captain of the Juniors. Being a Junior Firefighter taught Jonathan the basic firematic needs, allowed him the experience of being a volunteer firefighter and helping out his community. On the day of his seventeenth birthday, he became the youngest member to be voted into the Great Neck Vigilant Volunteer Fire Dept. Throughout his years at the Vigilant Fire Department, he, like his father before him, eventually rose to the rank of First Assistant Chief.

Jonathan's dad, Lee, was assigned to Rescue 2 in Brooklyn. Jonathan loved "buffing" with his father and went to work with him whenever the opportunity arose. He loved being with the firefighters, riding the rescue rig, and going to fires. He always told our family of his amazing adventures. One story was told to me a few years after it happened. One night Jonathan was riding with his dad and Rescue 2. It was the middle of the night and Rescue 2 was called to a 10-75 (working fire). The firefighters woke up when the bells sounded, except Jonathan. Rescue 2 was responding to the fire when the chauffeur looked out the rear view mirror and saw Jonathan running down the street with sneakers in hand. The men from Rescue 2 never let Jonathan forget that night. One of Jonathan's dreams was to become a member of Rescue 2, just like his dad. He was gaining experience within the New York City Fire Department and was very close to achieving his dream. He became a member of Squad 288 in Queens and eventually hoped to join Rescue 2.

There are not many people who love to go to work. Firefighters are a rare breed. Lee, Jonathan, and Brendan, who is presently assigned to Ladder 157 in Brooklyn, always and still love going to work. They all expressed their love for the job. Brendan, like his dad and brother, says he is going to "play," not work. Putting out fires and helping people in their great time of need was and still is their life's passion.

Aside from the births of his two sons, Andrew and Austin, Jonathan's happiest times were with the FDNY. Sitting at our dinner table and listening and watching Jonathan, Brendan, and Lee talk about their day at work was very comforting. Knowing my sons were so happy with their lives is a mother's dream.

Though his life was cut short on 9/11/01, Jonathan died doing what he loved so deeply, being a New York City firefighter.

Rest in peace, my son,
until we meet again.
Anne Ielpi

Robert F. Tipaldi

By Stella Lombardo,
Robert's mother

This is a story about a very special person, nicknamed "Little Big Man." It's not a fairytale, or a happily ever after story. It's a true story about my son, Robert Frank Tipaldi and it all started on May 6, 1976, the day he was born.

Robert was in such a hurry to get here that he was born a month early. For the first three months, he was a cranky little guy, always crying, but soon after, he began to adjust to his new life and surroundings. He had an older brother, Richard, who was willing to share all his toys with him. His childhood was pretty ordinary, I guess. They were two little boys, only 17 months apart, growing up, sharing, fighting, and protecting each other. When Robert was 4 ½ years old, I had my third child. Robert and Richard now had a baby sister named Lauren.

Robert was always more aggressive than his brother, and put up a fight for whatever he wanted. He loved teasing his little sister and sometimes made her cry. He kept himself busy and loved to play sports. At an early age, my boys started playing baseball. Then they moved on to football. They played for a couple of years, but Richard lost interest, and Robert was just too small to play against boys who were much bigger and stronger than him. Even though Robert was always short for his age, he would never let it get in the way of doing the things he wanted.

At school Robert had good grades, but got into trouble now and then. He was outspoken and always wanted to get in the last word. For that reason, I had many parent/teacher meetings and phone calls. He was popular with his friends, and was a very likeable boy. He just couldn't keep quiet in class. Although his teachers liked him, they did not appreciate his behavior in the classroom. He just always felt that be should be able to defend himself verbally if he was being accused of something he didn't do, or to disagree with something the teacher said. He was a handful, and yet so loveable. He was a cute boy with a beautiful smile, and it was hard to stay angry with him. By the time he entered sixth grade, he was getting blamed for most anything that happened at school, even if he wasn't involved. So, I decided to transfer him to another school in the 7th grade. He tried hard to improve his behavior and got along with everyone at the new school. He did well academically through 7th and 8th grade and graduated.

He went on to Xaverian High School where he made many more friends and joined the ice hockey team. He really loved playing ice hockey and continued to play ice and roller hockey during his adult life. Aside from the usual clowning around with his friends at school, Robert did well and graduated high school with honors. I was a very proud mom. He began to plan his future and started on his path to a successful career. He went to St John's University in Queens, NY and in January 1998, he graduated with a Bachelors Degree in Business.

Robert's personality basically remained the same even as an adult. He just loved to have fun. He continued to play sports. He had many close friends and was loyal to them. He loved his family and they meant the world to him. Robert learned from his mistakes and used these lessons in a positive way. He was a small man (5'3") with a big heart (thus nicknamed Little Big Man). He became a very caring, respectful, and giving young man.

Immediately after his college graduation, Robert started his career at Cantor Fitzgerald, a prestigious Wall Street brokerage firm. They were located at the World Trade Center. His office was on the 104th floor of the North Tower. He loved working there. He enjoyed the excitement and fast pace of the brokerage business. It was no surprise to his family that he was very well liked by his peers and upper management. He was moving swiftly up the ladder of success. He had a great job, and was loving life. He was 25 years old, single, living at home with me, his stepfather, brother, and sister. He had everything he wanted and he was on top of the world.

Then suddenly, without warning, his life ended tragically. On September 11, 2001, he left for work in the early morning. He and his brother traveled to work together each day. Robert went to his office and at 8:46 A.M. a plane hit the building. Robert immediately called to tell me what had happened. I could hear the fear in his voice as he described what was going on around him. The call only lasted a few minutes and it would be the last time I would ever hear from him again.

The whole world knows what happened that fateful day. Robert's life was lost and his remains were never found, but he continues to live in the hearts of all who knew him and loved him. He was a wonderful young man and his family will always be proud of him.

My life has changed dramatically since his death. When he died, he took a piece of my heart and left me with a treasure of memories. I have struggled emotionally to overcome the grief, and although it has been an uphill battle, my loss has taught me so much about life. I continue to surround myself with family and friends, and cherish the love and support given to me.

Although my family and I think of him everyday, we try to find a special way to celebrate his life each year. He will always be a part of our lives and he will always be our hero.

John "Pepe" Salerno

By Joann Cohn,
John's mother

My son, Pepe, lived life to the fullest. He was born with a smile on his face, which became contagious throughout his life. He would enter a room and all eyes would be on him because of his outgoing personality. He was full of vim and vigor and was so energetic, hence the nickname, Pepe. He was a tough little boy and at the same time was as gentle and caring as anyone could possibly be. You could always count on Pepe to make you laugh.

Pepe had a sister Dina, who was 2 1/2 years older. We also had dogs and cats, which Pepe was always loving and caring to. Our home was always the gathering spot for the neighborhood kids, and in general there was always stuff going on. The kids generally played outside and engaged in innocent fun which sometimes was a little bit scarier then I would have liked.

One day, when Pepe was about 4 years old, he decided to follow the dog to Waldbaums which was 2 blocks away. It took an hour to find him. When we finally found him, he and the dog were sitting in the window of the store eating a lollipop. He was laughing and smiling I was just so relieved I didn't know whether to kiss him or spank him. I should have realized then just how strong natured and confident Pepe was.

3 months old   6 yrs old   diving team show

St. John's Lacrosse game   Lacrosse

Our family life dramatically changed when Pepe's father and I got divorced. Pepe was about 6 years of age. He and Dina had to leave their friends and house and move into an apartment. As scary as this was to Pepe, it took no time for him to make new friends and start "clowning" around. We had a town pool around the corner and Pepe was on the diving team. One summer evening the team was putting on a show and Pepe had to dress like a clown. We dressed him in Dr. Dentons terry cloth pajamas with feet and a sideways baseball cap. Pepe made a beautiful dive into the pool but took a very long time to surface.

Michael and Pepe, NY Saints

Family—before Pepe left for London

Pepe—clowning around

Pepe and Michael on Pepe's birthday 9/6/2001.
Last picture of Pepe

The crowd was standing on their feet getting more nervous with time until finally he surfaced. He grabbed onto the side of the pool, smiling but needed assistance getting out. His costume weighed him down as the terry cloth got water-logged. Always the smile, never the fear, he looked at me and gave me a look like, "I'm ok, Mom."

Another change in Pepe's life occurred when he was 9 years old. I remarried and later had another son, Michael. My husband, Skip became a father and a role model. Pepe loved the idea of being the older brother and having a younger sibling to play with and prank. One day, they were wrestling and Michael's arm got broken. I'm not sure who felt worse Pepe or Michael. Pepe's friends would also come over and teach Michael to say things he shouldn't, it got Michael in lots of trouble. However, Pepe did teach Michael how to play lacrosse, which was one of Pepe's passions.

Pepe was more of an athlete then a scholar. He played lacrosse during high school and got a scholarship to Nassau Community and then a full scholarship to St. John's University. After graduation, he played a year on a professional team, the NY Saints. Pepe gave it his all, always.

Danielle and Jack (Pepe's son)

Dina's family (Dina, Jamie, Brielle, Ryan, and Morgan)

After college, in 1995, Pepe thought he was the luckiest guy in the world as he got a job with Cantor Fitzgerald as a foreign currency trader. It was amazing to me that my son who couldn't add in school was now in the financial world. He told me, "Mom, don't worry I use a calculator." I still grin when I think about it. Within 6 months, they offered him a position in London. He became engaged to his college sweetheart, Danielle, and moved to London. After they got married he transferred to Japan. While in Japan, Pepe sent me a card, thanking me for being his mom and helping him become the man he was and also how proud he was to be my son. That note, is the most treasured gift Pepe gave me and is my most prized possession. Pepe put his love of family first. His loving and caring nature became secondary.

In December, 2000, Pepe and Danielle finally moved back to the States and settled in Westfield, New Jersey. There was no doubt that my little boy had become a grown man. He took pride in his home and his lawn and there wasn't anything he wouldn't attempt to fix. He also volunteered to coach a boy's lacrosse team. He became a role model to those kids. They loved him and respected him and thought he was cool showing up to practice on his Harley. He taught those kids how to play lacrosse, but more importantly he taught them a life lesson. He took the time to compliment them on a good play and would tell them over and over that there is no "I" in team. Pepe lived by that—both on and off the field.

Pepe was beyond happy if such a word exists, the day he told us that Danielle and he were having a family of their own. He wanted as many kids as they could afford, as he would have been a terrific dad.

Then, on that horrific Tuesday, he and so many men and woman went to work, like any other day, but never came home. As a parent to watch that day unfold was by far the worst day of my life. The days that followed were a blur but our family had to find strength, as Danielle was pregnant and alone and needed our support. Our family changed forever that day. Whatever our "normal" was no longer existed.

March 1, 2002, was a new beginning for all of us as Jack Pepe Salerno was born. He was not only a blessing, but Jack gave us back what we so suddenly lost—a piece of his dad, Pepe. He is now 6 years old. Jack reminds us so much of Pepe and even though he never met his Daddy, he acts a lot like his Dad. He even raises his eyebrows the way his Daddy did. Jack hears stories about his Dad and refers to him as his "Daddy in Heaven." I know that Pepe is watching over him.

It is now almost 7 years since that tragic day. His sister, Dina now has three children, Morgan (9), Brielle (7), and Ryan (3). Jack has a brother, Harrison (1). Michael, Pepe's brother, is single. Not a day goes by that we don't think of Pepe a thousand times. I am so proud to have had Pepe as my son and cherish every day that we shared with him. Our time with him was not long enough but our fun times together have become beautiful memories that will live forever. He forever left a mark on our hearts, and touched all hearts he ever met.

Christopher Alexander Santora

By Alexander Santora,
Christopher's father

My son Christopher was the third child in our family of two older sisters and one younger. Seven years separated oldest from youngest, and all the babies grew up together. Chris was a "boy" as a child. Although surrounded with "girl stuff," (dolls, dresses, makeup, etc.) he was into cars, trucks, especially fire trucks, (which my grandchildren play with now), and action figures. He loved wrestling and the wrestling figures, star wars (he had the whole collection), He-Man figures, super heroes, etc. He could play for hours by himself and never stopped talking. On an interesting side note, my oldest grandson (also named Christopher after his uncle) is the carbon copy of my son in his play habits, actions, and the incessive talking. He also knows everything about being a fireman. (I can't figure out where he gets that from!)

I had often joked and said that Chris should become a lawyer because he certainly had the "gift of gab" as his Irish grandmother would say.

Chris always wanted a brother because he was "sick and tired" of all the girl stuff. When his mother Maureen was expecting our fourth child, Christopher prayed for a brother, one he could play with and wrestle with. When his sister Kathleen was born he was initially disappointed but quickly got over that. He accepted and loved his new baby sister.

64

Christopher and Kathleen

Al and Christopher

Christopher, college years

Kathleen, Jennifer, Santa, Megan, Patricia,
Christopher (bottom left, clockwise)

Christopher, Kathleen, Patricia, Jennifer, and Grand Mummy (clockwise)

Graduation Day
Christopher, Jennifer,
Megan (middle school grade 8)
Patricia (college),
Kathleen (high school),
Jada (friend) clockwise

Christopher, John (partially blocked),
Megan, and Patricia

Christopher and Megan

Patricia, Grand mummy (in back), Minnie Mouse, and Christopher

Tigger and Christopher Gramps, Christopher, and Al, Fire Academy 2001

A special kiss for my dear son College Graduation June 1999
Christopher & Mom   Al, Christopher & Maureen

We had friends that had three boys and Chris loved to hang out with them. He often said if he was to run away he would go to their house where only boys lived and they could do cool boy things (which they did) like burp, fart, and laugh about it. It was a much cooler place to be than our house which had three "yuckie" sisters with whom you could never do those things.

When Chris was fourteen, Maureen's sister, Kathleen died and left two children, Megan and Daniel. They came to live with us. Chris finally had the brother he always wanted. Although Daniel was 3 ½ and Megan was 5 ½ when they lost their mother, Christopher now had a brother and another sister. Daniel was much younger and somewhat physically challenged. He wore braces on his legs and was a sickly child from birth. Christopher would play with and entertain Daniel with the action figures, wrestling figures, and the Teenage Mutant Ninja Turtles that Daniel loved. Chris would put wrestling holds on Daniel and he would love that. At 14, Chris was still a big kid.

Chris wanted to become a cub scout, so guess who became the scout leader? You guessed it. I became the Scout Master for about six years as Chris and his friends grew up doing scout things. We camped, hiked, learned about compasses, built little soap box cars, and had a good time growing up. One time we went for a hike though the woods from the Boy Scout Camp in Alpine, New Jersey and got lost. Naturally, I couldn't let on that we were lost until after we found our way back. The other fathers knew it but the kids didn't. It's good to have compass skills; however you need to know where the town or destination lies. We found that out the hard way and laughed for many years.

Chris was a fierce competitor in everything he undertook. He loved skiing and basketball. When playing basketball he was faster than most players regardless of their size. At 5'7" he would have to be quicker to compensate for his size. Chris played basketball everyday after school in the playground in Queensview where we live. We live on the 11th floor facing the playground and it was without fail that you could hear my son yelling and sometimes cursing as he was playing ball. His mother would get so embarrassed and tell him on a regular basis not to yell or curse, but it was to no avail.

Chris was constantly telling jokes and playing tricks on everyone. Because of his antics, my little boy was endearingly called "Jokey Smurf" after the Smurf character on TV. He had outgrown an earlier name of "Hi Guy" which I dubbed him when he first began to talk; he picked it up from me when I would say "Hi Guy" to him. He started to repeat that phrase and it stuck for a few years.

Although Chris was not very big, he was very muscular. He was a very fast runner and did very well competing in track, but he thought it was boring. We signed him up for Little League and he participated playing various positions for about 10 years. That was grueling on the parents. A couple of afternoons and weekends for months on end (We thought it would never end!) we sat and watched the many baseball games. He not only played, but his sisters were in the Little League as well. We practically lived at that field. This was in addition to he and his sisters swimming at the YMCA, where they all learned to swim and when they were old enough, became life guards for many summers. Our children were never bored for lack of activities.

His sisters were enrolled in a local dancing school for years. When they were quite young we were required to purchase tap shoes for them. When Christopher saw them and heard the sound they made, he asked if he could go to dancing school too. Much to my chagrin we enrolled him in dancing. Little did we know that he only wanted the shoes because they made lots of noise. As soon as he got his tap shoes he announced that he no longer wanted to go to dancing school anymore. He put on his shoes and ran to the bathroom and taped on the tile floor to hear the noise. This became a big joke around our house for many years.

I was a pretty fair hand-ball player, having played from elementary school until recently. When Chris was about 15 years old, I challenged him to a game of handball. One Sunday afternoon, he ran me ragged and beat me two out of three games. A year or so later, we were visiting some friends in Montauk,

Long Island. While waiting for the food to be prepared for the picnic we shot some hoops and I was very impressed at his ability and agility. He was quite good at shooting and blocking. My little boy was no longer. He was becoming a man.

Christopher was given the gift of a photographic memory which enabled him to read something once and then recall what was read. The rule in our house was that homework had to be done before you could go out and play. This drove his sisters crazy, for they would still be doing homework while Chris was done and outside playing basketball.

My son was very bright and very verbal and opinionated. This got him into trouble in school. He had no tolerance for a teacher who was not prepared or didn't know his subject matter. In high school he realized if he worked a little, he would get into the honors classes, which he did. Those classes allowed greater latitude for the students, and Chris excelled. He had chosen to go to a high school which was 1 ½ hours away from the house. He had auditioned for the band, playing the clarinet which he learned to play in middle school. He enjoyed playing while in school, and continued to practice and play at home after he graduated.

At 16 Chris used his swimming skills to get a part time job as a lifeguard at a local tennis club. Chris loved this job which didn't require much effort (not too many people went into the water.) He would schmooze the members by getting them towels and setting up the chaise lounges wherever they wanted them to be placed. He was rewarded by receiving nice tips. His sisters, who also worked there, didn't do as well. Their attitude was very different—if someone wanted a towel they would show the person where they could get one. They couldn't understand why Chris did so much better financially.

Christopher graduated Queens College with a degree in History. American History was his passion. He loved reading facts, so history was a natural with all the dates and times of events. Christopher taught as a substitute teacher in several schools in Astoria. He was a good teacher and the kids related to him well. He would work sports into his lessons and could communicate with the kids on their level. One lesson I remember him preparing and talking about was the Civil War and how he related it to the Super Bowl. Christopher was offered a permanent position at an intermediate school which he refused because he knew be was going to be called by the Fire Department early in 2001. He didn't want to start the school semester and then have to leave in the middle of it. In January 2001 he was notified that be would be in the first class of the Fire Academy. He had studied and trained for about a year which paid off. He achieved perfect scores in both the written and the physical exams. The test for the FDNY is very competitive and unless you achieve a high score, your chance of being called is remote.

Well Chris had achieved his dream of becoming a firefighter. He absolutely loved his job, perhaps because there were no women, at least in the house he was in. His permanent assignment was Engine Company 54, quartered with Ladder 4 and Battalion 9 on 8th Avenue and 48th Street in Manhattan.

On September 11, 2001, Christopher had worked the night before and was due to come home. My 23 year old son never came home. He perished that day along with the 14 other "brothers" from his firehouse. Engine 54, Ladder 4, Battalion 9 lost all 15 members that day, more than any other regular house in the city. The FDNY lost 343 members that horrific day, 18 of them Probationary firefighters from the 1st class from the new list, and my only son Christopher was one of them.

My son Christopher Alexander Santora is a very special and dear person to me. I love my son very much and miss him everyday. As I pondered what to write about, I was perplexed. How do I explain what is in my heart, mind, and soul regarding my dead son, my only son, who I didn't hug enough (guys don't do that), and didn't tell I loved him enough (that's sissy stuff)? Now that he is gone I will never be able to see him in this life and tell him these things, although I do everyday in my prayers. I only hope he knows these things. I would advise all fathers, don't be squeamish about giving your sons a hug and telling them that you love them (It's not only for girls.) Do it every day, because as I found out, your life and the lives of your loved ones can change in a heartbeat. Don't have regrets; they are haunting. Here's to you, Chris, I will never forget you. You are in my heart and mind. I love you son, now and forever.

Love,
DAD

* * *

The following memories were written by Christopher Santora's sisters:

Christopher was the third child in our family and the only boy. He was the best brother a girl could ever have asked for. Despite the times we may have disagreed, Christopher always had my best interest in mid. He was devoted to his family and always put his family first. There was nothing that he could not do. He was a daredevil and he tried everything. I remember when we were on our family vacation going across the United States. We went to many of the National parks. One of the many excursions we had was a boat ride down the Colorado River. It was called the lazy boat ride because it was just a scenic ride at a slow pace. The driver stopped the boat at one point and had asked if anyone wanted to take a dip in the river; he also mentioned that the river was very cold (approximately 55°F). Well my brother couldn't pass up the opportunity. He went on about the river's temperature saying that it wasn't cold and he was going to swim around for a bit. He jumped in and immediately jumped out. We were all laughing so hard while he was just sitting there shivering, saying it was freezing like jumping into a bucket of ice cubes.

I have so many memories of my brother. He was always joking around and could make anyone laugh. He loved music of all types and he and I went to several concerts together. He was smart and very interested in current events and world history. He was easy to talk to and one of the most kind-hearted people I believe I will ever know. Even now as I write this, tears fill my eyes. We lost our brother too early. Not a day goes by that he is not in my thoughts. I loved my brother and miss him dearly.

Love, Jennifer Echevarria—Christopher's oldest sister

*   *   *

As I sit here trying to think of a memory of my brother, Christopher A. Santora, so many come to mind. He was truly one of a kind. He was smart, funny and confident. He knew he had great qualities, which made him sort of cocky. Where that trait might have turned some people off, it also drew so many in. He had a kind of personality that people wanted to be around. In school it made him the class clown, and as an adult he was the life of the party. He could always make light of a situation. He didn't want people to fight, and thus became the peace maker. He really was a wonderful, all-around guy. The world is so unfortunate to not have him here anymore. Who knows how many other lives he would have touched? Anyone who knew him was privileged.

One particular occasion, when he was just about 20, he was driving home with a few of his friends. Chris didn't have a fancy car. It was kind of old and ugly, but it got him around and to him this was great. He was glad to have a car because he was able to hang out and go places. Just as he was about to turn onto our block, a drunken man who was having some sort of fight with whoever he lived with threw a brick at Chris' car. It hit the hood of his car and left a big dent. Chris, who was about to turn left, put the car into park and flung his door open. He left the car running and his two friends in the car and got out of the car like a raging lunatic. He chased this guy to his door, which was across the street next to the candy store. All awhile, he was yelling and cursing like a madman. You can imagine what he was screaming. This drunken man must have seen this lunatic after him, and he ran into his house. Chris started to bang and pound on his door. Now mind you, his car was still running in the middle of the street with the driver's door open. This was creating a scene in the street because by now the whole neighborhood was out and it was creating a traffic jam. "Come out here you f$%&!@# a! #$%#$. I'm going to f#$%@#$ kill you!" You could only imagine the rest of what he was saying. Those of us who were witness to this were so hysterical, we almost wet our pants. This only made Chris even more mad. Someone called the cops. When they got there, the bystanders told them what had happened. The cops wanted to talk to the guy in the house. When he finally came to the door, he told them, "This guy is after me, he's pounding on my door." The cops told the guy that he was lucky that he didn't get killed. In the end, nothing happened to Chris, other than his ugly brown car getting yet another dent, and for us to have this hysterical memory of a typical "Chris."

I miss my brother everyday. He was not only my brother, but my best buddy as well. I miss going out with him, and hanging out, laughing and having fun. Going out with Chris always meant a good time.

But he also had a serious side. He valued my opinion, he wanted my approval, and for my little brother who looked up to me, I cherish that.

Just before he died, actually a few months before, I met his girlfriend. They had been dating for sometime, but Chris would only bring a girl around when it was serious. I knew he liked this girl a lot; he loved her. He wanted to get my opinion of her before he proceeded with his relationship. That was very endearing. One day she was at the house, and although we didn't really talk, I sized her up. Later that night, he asked "P, what did you think of her?" I said, "She's nice, she's pretty, but I don't like her white eyeliner." Well time went on, and that horrible day occurred. I since have become one of her best friends. We were there for each other, and I felt it was my obligation to make sure she was OK in dealing with his death. That made us very close and she even became my son's godmother. Well I later found out that in fact Chris had told her, "My sister doesn't like your white eye makeup, don't wear it again." Now years later, I am still mortified that my brother was so blunt . . . but it makes me smile.

I love you Chris! . . . . Until we meet again.

Your loving sister
Patricia Santora Cardona—Christopher's second older sister

*   *   *

My brother Christopher has been called many things: brave, strong, courageous, hero, to name a few. But before be was any of these things, he was my brother. My *big* brother. The term big brother is synonymous with many things, none of which include the attributes he has come to be known as. Bully, tattletale, meanie, and fart-king are far better descriptions of big brothers. Before my brother was out saving lives and risking his in the process, he was busy making my life as miserable as he could.

When we were growing up, I looked up to my brother for everything. He knew this, of course, and with this knowledge he did the only thing any big brother could do; take advantage of it. He would crouch around the corners of our apartment, waiting for me to unsuspectingly come his way. With a menacing shriek he would leap into view, nearly scaring me to death. He would slide his socked feet on the carpet, charging his two pointer fingers with enough static electricity to shock the daylights out of me. He would threaten me with a freshly-picked booger, waving it tauntingly so as a constant reminder of my consequence should I decide to tell dad that he was holding my beloved teddy bear hostage. On long car trips he would amuse himself by putting his finger as close to my face as humanly possible, responding to my complaints by claiming that he was not touching me. He would persuade me time and time again to play one of his favorite games, "yes means no and no means yes", knowing I would diligently follow the rules. It took me a long time to figure out that he only followed the rules when it was in his advantage, and in doing so was able to trick me into admitting I was a boy, a crybaby, a hairy ape, etc and that he was the best-at-everything, king of the world, coolest in the car, etc.

Of all the big-brotherly stunts and devious accomplishments he patted himself on the back for, my brother was most proud of his role as creator and enforcer of my fear of mannequins. The idea actually started from my two older sisters, who had somehow discovered how terrifying our nude, headless Barbie dolls could appear to an innocent four year old (I was also a victim of the evil, older-sister-tag-team, whose antics were strikingly similar to that of the mean big brother, now that I think about it.) This bizarre torment took place almost every time we played, and always ended with me being backed into a corner as the big-headed-bully-brigade marched slowly toward me, armed to the teeth with Barbies without heads or clothes.

I imagine that during one of our very regular trips to Macy's or K-Mart, my brother (who was always on the hunt for new material) must have made the discovery that mannequins, particularly the headless ones, have a stark resemblance to the dreaded Barbie dolls. The only difference was, of course, that the mannequins were life-sized and would therefore inflict terror on a much greater scale. I imagine he must have been so pleased with his cunning prowess to have devised such a plan; what could possibly be better than to take a pre-existing fear and intensify it to colossal size?

One day while we were trailing our mom in a department store, my brother came very close to me and whispered into my ear, "When all the lights are out and the store is closed, all the mannequins come to life, and if you don't behave, I'm going to lock you in here"

I quickened my pace and remained at my mother's side, and with each whine or complaint that I was bored or tired, I would be met by the chin-down, eyebrows-raised look of my brother, reminding me to zip it or else. He even made up a little song and would mouth the words from across the aisles: "The mannequins are gonna get you . . . the mannequins are gonna get you . . ." and keep me in a constant state of trepidation. I became paranoid that the mannequins were following me with their eyes, hungry to snack on a small brown-haired girl in the dark. I would walk the aisles of J.C. Penny in the exact center, afraid to get too close on one side or the other out of fear that a mannequin might grab me with a cold, plastic hand. I was always watching my back and extra careful never, ever to get lost from our parents.

In this very same manner I was tormented for years and my anxiety was intensified by the fact that I actually believed my brother. Whereas after time I grew strong enough to stand up against the deranged Barbie ritual, the fear of mannequins remained intact for a long time. I think it was the seriousness in my brother's face and the grave tone he would use when reminding me what would happen if I misbehaved that made it all the more frightening. It was the way that he would come very close and whisper (as if he didn't want the mannequins to know their secret was out) that made me dread accompanying my mom to the store.

Now when I am shopping at a department store I can't help but think of all this and laugh. I have to give him the credit he deserves for managing to scare the wits out of me for all those years. I have to hand it to him for never once laughing or otherwise indicating that it was all a hoax. Even as adults, he never confessed to me that it was just a prank, a joke, a trick he devised as a cruel big brother. There is no other ten year old in the world who could have delivered a more believable performance. I look at the mannequins now and get misty eyed, thinking of my brother and his eternal meanness and wishing he was here so I could try to get him back in some sort of way. I think of how clever and funny my brother was when I pass one of those plastic dummies, and I smile—smile and quicken my pace, careful to avoid eye contact at all cost.

I love you Chris!
Kathleen Santora-Christopher's first little sister

*   *   *

My Brother Christopher was the only boy in a family of girls. He wanted nothing more then to have a baby brother. When my mom was pregnant with her fourth child and then I came along, Christopher said prayers that we were boys. He wasn't so lucky.

My family went on a lot of family vacations together, one more memorable than the next. They would all start out pretty much the same. There was always one person that was not ready on time. It was usually Christopher. Each time my dad would tell him, "WE ARE GOING TO LEAVE WITHOUT YOU! You have five minutes and that is it!" We never did leave him.

The first time my family went on a cruise, we went snorkeling. Christopher decided to take bread from breakfast to feed the fish. By the time we arrived at the beach, he had long forgotten about the bread in his pockets, and was "attacked" by the fish!

When Christopher was in High School he started working as a lifeguard at this private club. I will never forget all the times we went swimming there. I was always treated like gold because everyone loved Chris! He often re-arranged his plans to take me to a school dance or include me when he went to the movies with his friends. He didn't have to include me in anything, but he did because that was the kind of person he was.

As Christopher got older, he realized that having four sisters wasn't so bad, especially when it came to doing his chores. He would often beg and plead with us until one of us finally gave in and did them. My sisters and I often did the dishes and all kinds of household chores. I was smarter than my sisters because I got Chris to pay me for doing his laundry and ironing his clothes. When Christopher was in the Fire Academy, he came home the first day begging me to help him. He needed me to help iron his uniform and make creases. I helped him and he paid me, too!!

Christopher made it his business to teach at least one of his sisters about sports. I was the only one who was interested. My brother was the biggest sports fan I knew. His love and interest in sports has worn off on me. Now, when I am watching a game I often picture Christopher sitting next to me watching it too.

I will always love Christopher even through we didn't always get along. In fact, most of time, we were at each other's throats. I will always remember those times. They showed me that he cared enough about me to have the argument in the first place.

My brother Christopher will forever be in my heart and with me always. I love you Chris!

Love
Megan Santora—Christopher's baby sister

Michael Andrew Tamuccio

By Patricia Ellen and James William Tamuccio Sr,
Michael's parents

Who is Michael? You ask, but there is no easy answer. Michael Andrew was our first born. A charming little boy whose first word at ten months of age, believe it or not (we almost couldn't believe it) was "dinosaur." He was a normal boy with ups and downs who grew up to be an exceptional young man—strong, handsome, giving, and loving. It was always a wonder to us how our shy, timid little guy grew into the strong, take-charge man that he was.

He was a typical teenage boy—full of energy and ideas. He was an exceptional student with the gifts of both a retentive and photogenic mind. He was an avid athlete from the time he was six or seven years old—think he played every sport you could think of, except football. Ice hockey, baseball, and wrestling were his sports and he excelled at them all. He was a member of the Nassau County All Star traveling hockey team and we traveled all over with him. He was a very focused young man and did very well in school. He attended Chaminade High School in Mineola, New York, where he set a record for a 9 second pin in wrestling—not sure if it was ever broken.

Michael was a member of our parish Boy Scout troop and was nearing the time when he should have been going for his Eagle Scout award. He had an Assistant Scout Master that really rode him hard, so for the longest time he would avoid working on earning his Eagle Scout award. As he neared the age deadline, which I believe was 17, the Assistant Scout Master would really taunt him and of course, Michael continued to dig his heels in. We could not make him see the light of day and how important this award could be for his future. He and his boyhood friend Frankie, along with Frankie's brother Genie, were determined they were not going to give in. How and when the light bulb went off for them is a mystery to us all, but all of sudden with the age deadline looming in front of them, they decided to go for it.

Michael campaigned for the hospice program at Mercy Hospital—his grandfather had been one of the first patients in the hospice program there. With the Assistant Scout Master breathing down their necks—taunting them about not making the deadline, they bore down and made it by the skin of their teeth. They were all good boys but, as with most boys, if you rubbed them the wrong way, they would go the other way.

East Meadow Little League
1974 All Star Team
Front row, left to right
2nd in—Michael—Catcher's gear

Michael, 1974,
All Star Team Catcher

Bellmore Hockey League, 1977

Michael at bat, 1974

On one occasion during that infamous senior year of high school, the boys all wore tuxedos to school and were going to have a special farewell lunch. It was the last day of classes before final exams began and the last meal they would be sharing there—they compared it to The Last Supper (blasphemous, I'm sure you're thinking.) Well, their formal dress was taken as an insult to the brothers who thought they were making fun of them (they always wore black suits.) They all were told to go home and come back in proper school attire within two hours—anyone who wasn't back within that time frame would be suspended, forbidden from the prom and from participation in the graduation exercises! As parents, we were very upset but did have a chuckle or two—after all, it was an all boys high school and they were bound to act up occasionally. I think we all let out deep breaths when graduation day finally arrived!!

Jimmy & Michael

Chaminade High School, Record Maker,
9 Second Pin

Chaminade High School, 1982
WrestlingTeam, 125 weight class

Eagle Scout Award, 1981
Right to left: James Tamuccio, Sr., Patricia
Tamuccio, Michael Andrew Tamuccio

Chaminade High School was a very structured environment that would bring out, every now and then, the rebel that every teenage boy has inside of them. They would pull pranks on each other and on the brothers and sometimes would get into hot water. One occasion that comes to mind is when Michael was a senior in high school—his best bud Tommy had written on the carpet in one of the classrooms, "Hooray—can't wait to be out of here!" Well, somehow it was discovered by one of the brothers and all students that had been in that classroom were interrogated. Michael was a most loyal friend and of course was not going to be charged with being the rat that turned his buddy in. He underwent a grueling interrogation but wouldn't bend—even under the threat of suspension and expulsion and of behaving "un-Christian like." Tommy eventually fessed up and boy did they all pay. But to Michael, his friend was most important and his loyalty to Tom came before his own fate. This is who Michael was—if nothing else he was a true friend—something that stayed with him all his life.

Michael Andrew Tamuccio was a complex person—a loving and devoted son, and leader within his peer group. A brother who cared—sometimes too much, his brother Jimmy and sister Dana would say, trying to be fatherly as well as brotherly. He took care of things—if he said he was going to do something, he would—if he asked you to do something, he expected it to be done. He was a good husband and friend to his wife Kathleen but was never afforded the opportunity to be a good dad, which I know he would have been. In the short 31 years that he was given, he had experienced much and had enjoyed life to the fullest. Though his time had been limited, he left this world having accomplished most of what he had wanted to do and fulfilling the dreams that he had as a youngster—for that we are grateful and thank God. Michael had fought to come into this world of ours, and left it in a most tragic and sudden way—all because he was an American seeking to fulfill the American dream—why this was his destiny and the destiny of almost 3,000 others is something only God can answer.

* * *

My Brother, Mike Tamuccio

My brother Michael was the most intelligent, dedicated, and driven man I have ever known. He routinely went out of his way to help and inspire those that were around him, whether it be in business or in sports. Michael gave many people their first shot on Wall Street and when some felt that they were not up to the task, he always believed in them and did whatever it took to help that person succeed.

As Michael and I grew up, I was always in competition with him, yet he was never in competition with me. When we were young, he always told me that I was the better athlete, but I never believed him because he was always in the league or age group ahead of me.

In 1992, Michael, who had been playing in men's ice hockey leagues for years, had moved to a new team with a few friends. He told the coach that the only way he would play was if his little brother could join the league too. I had not played ice hockey competitively in ten years. I had to continually remind him of that fact. Michael would not take no for an answer. So I reluctantly joined the team to play for the first time as my brother's team mate.

A few seasons passed and our team, "The Hogs", improved to where we made it into the league finals. During that season, with my brother's help as my right wing, I led the team in scoring. As the game went on, we were losing 2-1, and during the break between the second and third periods, my brother decided that I needed a kick in the pants because I was not playing up to my potential. Because of the magnitude of the game, I was very nervous. He took me to the edge of the bench, and told me that I was more of a natural athlete than he was and that

I should just relax. He asked me what I needed to loosen up. And at that point, I lifted my head and felt a sense of calm and belief that I had not felt all night. As we looked into each other's eyes, he gave me that sly grin of his and gave me a head-butt. I then told him that he gave me just what I needed, the belief and strength in myself that he always had in me. As we went back to play the third period, my brother worked his butt off to get the puck to me. With only minutes to play, I scored the tying goal!! I had never seen my brother so pumped up.

Just before we started the overtime period, my brother kept talking in my ear, telling me that it was up to us; if we wanted it, then we were going to have to go and take it. As the period ground on, my brother was working the right boards against a much larger guy. I did not think he had a shot at getting the puck out, but just as I crossed the red line, I saw my brother look over his right shoulder and smile. And sure enough, he got the puck out to me. I took it all the way in and scored the game's wining goal. As I turned with arms raised high, the first person that I saw was my brother Mike grinning from ear to ear, screaming, "You did it! You did it! You did it!" as he tackled me to the ice in pure excitement at having won the championship together. But in my mind, I knew that I would not have been able to overcome my faults and fears without his constant and never wavering belief in me.

To this day, almost fourteen years later, it is one of my most cherished memories of my brother and only a small window or picture of the effects that my brother Michael had on me. Even though he is no longer physically here, whenever I have doubt, fear, or just want to give up, I close my eyes and think of my brother and how much he loved me and how he never quit or gave up on me.

Michael—I just want to say thank you for all your love and the passion you instilled in me.

Love always, your little brother,
Jimmy

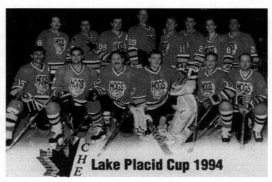

Championship Game 1994
Front row, left to right: Jimmy and Michael Tamuccio

*   *   *

Mike 'Moocha' Tammucio
Through The Eyes Of His Boyhood Buddy, Frank Cioffi

Camping in my backyard with Michael aka 'Moocha' aka 'the Mooch'
Tamuccio (As remembered by Frank Cioffi—best buds since they were
3 years old)

Michael was my best friend growing up and we had one especially good
summer together. We were around eleven or twelve years old when Mike's Dad
got him a used tent. It was a classic wall tent and it was pretty big; at our age
we could stand up in it easily and it had plenty of room for us to sleep in. I
had an in-ground pool so we decided to do a sleep over in my yard. The tent
was too big and heavy for us to move on our bikes, so Mr. Tamuccio dropped
it off and we set it up in my yard over a small patio that my dad had put in for
the picnic table. Then we got our sleeping bags, clothes, and towels into the
tent and that is the way it started. We were only supposed to sleep there one
night and by the time we got set up half the day was over. We spent the rest
of the day in the pool trying to do flips off of the diving board and playing
"destroyers and depth charges." This game involved the inner tubes my dad
had gotten from work. Everybody started in a tube in the pool except one
person. The idea was to jump feet first from the side of the pool and land on
the tube, flipping the tube and the guy in it over. If you stayed in you kept
going, if not you became a depth charge. The last guy in a tube won. The
Mooch weighed about a hundred pounds soaking wet so he was easy to flip
and when he came after you he had a hard time flipping you over. His little
brother Jimmy had it worse because he weighed half that, but that didn't stop
him from trying. This went on all day and into the night. We stopped for
dinner and cooked hotdogs on the grill outside. Swimming at night was a
treat because the water was warmer then the air, but we had to keep it down
so we shifted to Marco Polo. My Mom turned off the flood lights to signal
it was time to go to bed so we dried off the best we could with our already
soaked towels and turned in. Not that we were going to sleep, but we tried
to. That is when the Bugs Bunny arguments began. We all had our favorite
cartoons and lines. The Mooch was a big fan of the "Monster" cartoons but
we all agreed the WW2 reference cartoons were the best. None of us had
ever seen an A card but we got it.

The next day we ate cereal outside and then started a whiffleball game in my
driveway that morphed into a neighborhood tournament. Mike and I were of
course on the same team and our little brothers just had to deal with it. The other

kids from the neighborhood showed up and started calling winners. A single was anything that got past the curb. A double was past the curb on a fly. A triple had to clear the center line on the street and a home run had to clear the far curb or hit the branches of the red maples that grew on that side of the street. The ball had to stay between the house numbers painted on the curb on the left and the fire hydrant across the street on the right to be fair. I had a pitch back with a red ribbon strike zone on it that did all the catching. My driveway sloped down just enough to roll the ball all the way back to the pitcher. It was the perfect field and Mike and I took on all comers. We even did a number on the bigger kids. We figured out who pitched to who best and just went with that. When it got too hot to play any more we just jumped into the pool and went at it.

Some of the other kids came with us and while we were playing, Mike accidentally knocked Danny Stiegerwalt's front tooth out with his elbow. Danny lived across the street and was a huge Islander fan. He had a handicapped arm but that didn't stop him from playing anything, and he was the best and toughest on our street hockey team. Danny didn't even get mad because he had hurt that tooth before and just kind of pushed it back in. He thought he looked like a real hockey player now so after it stopped bleeding he jumped back into the pool and dunked Mike a couple of times just on principle. Again we had hot dogs and everybody stayed late and wanted to sleep in the tent but my mom sent everybody home except Mike and Jimmy. We pretty much repeated that day the whole week. Our parents were fine with it and all we needed every day was another pack of hotdogs. We even got out of going to church on Sunday. Moocha was a born athlete so he always wanted to play a sport and that was fine because we were all into it. We played everything from touch football in the street to chip and putt in my backyard.

Then we got our skateboards out and Mike had his accident. This was when skateboards were just coming out with urethane wheels and they were made of fiberglass. One of the early tricks was to ride tandem with another skater on two boards. You would sit on your board and the other guy would sit on his facing each other. Then you would put your feet on the other guy's board and hold onto each others arms. You needed a hill to go down, and the next block over had one. My little brother Gene and Mike had done it before and they were pretty good at it. Then one time they tried to turn on some sand while they were going pretty fast and wiped out. This was back in the seventies, way before helmets or any other type of padding were popular. Mike landed on his shoulder and skidded along the pavement pretty good. He came up a bloody mess and my mom had to patch him and my brother up. That didn't stop us though, and of course since it was the seventies, the chlorine was good for wounds so it was back into the pool. We had another good day even with Mike's shoulder hurting him until a storm rolled in at night. This was a heck of a storm and to our surprise, but not our parents, the tent

Right to left
Michael, Frankie, Gene, and Jimmy

leaked. We would have been fine even though we were getting a little wet until the wind really picked up and it started to thunder. My dad came out and got us and we ended up in the basement, soaked. Mom got us dry clothing and a bunch of blankets

Rained Out, 1972
Right to left
Michael, Frankie, Gene, and Jimmy

Camping in the Yard, 1972
Left to right
Michael, Frankie, Gene, and Jimmy

and we settled in to the standard argument. In the morning we discovered the tent had blown down and everything was wet so we called it quits. We figured we had forever to do it again but we never really did. We went to summer camp together with the scouts every year after that and that was just as good if not better.

A lot of people don't really know how Moocha got his nick name. His last name was Tamuccio and you would think that was it, but that was only part of it. When we were thirteen or so we experimented with cigarettes and Mike liked 'em. The thing was he was really scared of his dad finding out and getting caught with a pack, so he never bought them for himself. He was always looking to mooch one off you, so guys used to say, "Here comes the Moocha" and reach for their smokes. His standard pickup line with the girls when we got older was to ask for a butt. So that was how he got his nickname and then it got shortened to just Mooch.

My son is seven now and his favorite is when Bugs Bunny keeps tricking Daffy Duck into telling Elmer Fudd to "Shoot me now!" Of course Elmer blasts him and his bill ends up in a different place each time. With any luck, one day in the pouring rain I'll have to walk across my yard, flashlight in hand, to the tent with all the laughter coming from it. I mean really, somebody has to argue for the monster.

*   *   *

WHEN WE WERE YOUNG—Michael and Colleen

When we are young, almost all of us believe that we will live forever and that our future is bright and secure. We don't imagine a world of sorrow or danger. We hope that our friends and family will stay with us always and that our life can make a difference to those that we know and love. What we don't realize is that despite losing touch with family and friends or going in different directions in life, the bonds that we make during our early years actually do stay with us forever. For me, there is no more perfect example of this than Michael Tamuccio.

I first remember Michael back in junior high school. I had recently lost my mother and my friends were the only source in my life that gave me happiness and hope. It was a difficult time to say the least. I did my best to hide what I was going through—my friends didn't ever realize my mother was sick—because I wanted at least that part of my life to be happy and sorrow free. I wasn't sure how I was going to become the person that I wanted to be without the love and support of my mother, who held my family together. Despite all the odds, I was confident that I would do everything I could to live as normal of a life as possible and reach my goals, regardless of my situation. How I was to do that, I wasn't quite sure. Enter Michael Tamuccio.

Michael was the sort of friend that you just knew was genuine. He had a very deep love for his family, which at that age wasn't something most of our friends would easily admit. He was very grateful for everything they had given him and that was why it was important to Michael to make them proud. Michael believed in hard work and dedication, whether it was by his long time commitment as an Eagle Scout, to his school work, or his friends. He gave you the sense that nothing was important if you didn't work hard enough to achieve it. You just knew that Michael would do well in whatever he chose to do with his life. He was the rock, the voice of wisdom amongst us silly teens, and the one that you could always count on. He was just a unique brand of special.

I remember vividly one night when we were all together, Michael pulled me aside and told me something that would change my life. He told me how much he admired how I could persevere in keeping my life together despite losing my mother. He was emotional just thinking about if the situation was reversed because his family meant everything to him. He told me that I should be proud of coming so far and that he knew that I would continue to do so despite whatever odds. He never doubted my abilities. He had faith in me. He told me my defiance to beat these odds was a testament to my mother and that her spirit would help me get through—I just had to listen.

Up until that night, no one had even acknowledged my struggles, not to mention my accomplishments. When everyone else was more comfortable not talking about what was obvious, Michael was quick to lend me a shoulder and build up my spirit. That night set the tone for the rest of my adult life and I never forgot what he said.

It's true that when you get older, you sometimes outgrow your friends. Life becomes complicated and despite efforts, you sometimes lose touch with those you care most about. I remember how proud and sad I was when Michael went off to college. He was moving on and away. Although we stayed in touch for the first year, we had fallen out of touch by the year he graduated when ironically, I entered the same college. I remember thinking that I had made Michael proud that I too could go to the same school that he did. I thought about how that conversation that one night as a teen helped me to reach that goal. I'd occasionally miss him at a Yankee game or look for him around the World Trade Center where he worked when I lived in Battery Park City. I would be kept awake at night by the humming of the Twin Towers and the light that was cast 24/7 in my bedroom by all the late night workers. It felt that he was around even though it had been a long time.

September 11th, 2001 was inarguably the most tragic day the world has ever seen, at least in my 43 years. Everyone, everywhere had their eyes focused at Ground Zero. How could any of us survive such a great loss? Like most of us at first, I had no idea that Michael hadn't made it to safety. It had been so long since we spoke; I just assumed that someone as loving, compassionate, and genuine as Michael could not have possibly suffered in that way. The world needed him. He was too important. When the lists started to hit the internet I was in the midst of taking care of my sister who was in a coma. We shut off the TV to keep her from hearing about how the world was falling to pieces. I had no idea who was lost that day until the paper came and I saw Michael's name. A million things went through my mind—It shouldn't have been him—Why someone so gifted and loving? Why didn't I return that last call? How in the world can his family cope with this? For years I couldn't even bring myself to talk about Michael or September 11th. It was too painful. My friends and family worried about why I couldn't move on from this tragedy. I have had my fair share of losses—my sister passed three weeks after September 11th and my father the following year to the day—but for some reason, I couldn't let Michael go.

As an avid runner, I would get up most mornings and do my daily run by the ocean. It was where I would go to make sense of things, but since September 11th, even my runs were uninspiring. One particular morning, I awoke just before sunrise and decided to get an early start before my newborn son would take over me for the day. As I was running and drowning out my panting with inaudible, loud music, I heard something call to me, "Hey Colleen, watch how beautiful the sunrise is going to be today. Turn off your head phones and listen to the morning birds and waves crashing. Don't overlook the beauty that's around you today." In recent years, I have become much less faithful and I normally don't buy into signs such as this, but this wasn't an ordinary voice. It was loud and clear. It was Michael.

Since then, he would join me on my runs and listen to my problems and we'd always end up with him showing me something about life that I had been missing. It meant so much to me to feel like I could connect with him in some way. For so long I just couldn't bring myself to move on from that day. I'd think about his friends and family, and most importantly, his mom.

Sunrise run morning of 9-11-01

Freedom Flight

On the fifth anniversary of September 11th I left a brief message thanking my friend for being in my life and for allowing me to enjoy the beauty of a sunrise. Almost immediately after the post, I received an email from Michael's mother, Mrs. T. She was touched by the post and wanted to know how I knew her Michael. She was learning more and more about the many people whose lives were touched by Michael and even in his passing, continue to be. I was so honored to have heard from her. What if in some very small way, I could provide her with a memory of Michael that she didn't have before? What if in doing so she can share with me more about his life that I had missed? It wasn't very long after we started to communicate that I felt like Mrs. T. was someone I had always known and someone I would always want to be part of my life. I had begun to heal because she helped me to do so and when I think of how unselfish that is, considering it was her beloved son that was lost, I am reminded again that this is Michael's mother. I should have expected nothing less.

Michael once again has given me one of the most important gifts I have ever received. One person's life truly can make a difference and even when they are physically gone they are still with you forever. You just need to listen. They are all around giving us signs. Michael, my friend, you have given me a renewed sense of faith, much like that night in our teens. You continue to give even in your passing. How typical, Michael. You and your family will always be in my heart. Thank you for bringing back joy into my life.

By Colleen Horan-Green

Christopher Paul Slattery

By Erin Slattery Appelle,
Christopher's sister

It's funny how relationships change with time. Chris and I were two and a half years apart and growing up we spent a lot of time playing together, whether it was digging to China in the backyard, or sitting in the back of the Oldsmobile driving for 7 hours to a ski mountain in Vermont. Did we fight? Of course we did, but we were also best friends without realizing it. It probably wasn't until our oldest brother, Dan, left for college that we realized it and by then we were 14 and 16 ½ years old.

Now when we were younger, I was usually the one to tattle since I was the youngest and the only girl, plus I would certainly lose in a physical battle with 2 older brothers. However this once, Chris and I got into an argument about something or other and I hit him. With a wry smile, he looked at me and said, "I'm going to tell Mom." I remember the sinking feeling of fear, but I also recall thinking that I wasn't going to let him get away with it, especially since he clearly wasn't in pain. Away he ran up the stairs and within minutes he was returning down the stairs with a grin, melodiously calling, "Erin, Mom wants you!" Before he sang out my name, I gathered a plan which included one of his Tonka trucks. I stood waiting around the corner at the bottom of the stairs with my sweaty palms tightly gripping his truck. As his toe struck the bottom stair and he began calling out a second time, "Erin, Mom . . ." WHACK! I had come around the corner and belted him full force in the stomach with the truck. Being two and a half years younger, the small hit I had given him earlier left him with a smile. However, this time he howled and Mom came running!

As we got older, the physical parts of the arguments diminished, but we still had our moments when Mom would send us each to our rooms in disgust. Our bedrooms were right next to each other, so when she sent us up there we had to walk up the stairs together and refrain from continuing the argument. It was funny because in the short 10 steps up to our rooms, the anger would subside, and by the time we got to our rooms we would keep our doors open and sit on the metal dividers that separated each of our rooms from the carpet of the hallway, laughing about what had happened. When my mother realized that we

Chris at 2 ½
(at brother Dan's birthday party)

Chris and Erin winning July 4th
Block Party competition

Chris and Erin musical duet

Teenager Chris

High School graduation with brother Dan and
good friends Robbie and Joe (Chris on right)

were enjoying ourselves while we should have been deep in our misery sulking in our individual rooms, she insisted we shut our doors. A wall was not going to stop Chris. Suddenly I heard a slight three taps on the wall and when I didn't immediately answer, it came again. I left my bed and echoed it, "Tap, tap, tap."

From the other side there was silence but I knew it was his way of saying, "Hey, I'm still here." From then on, our wall tapping became a type of Morse code that only he and I understood.

When I was starting high school and Chris was going to be a junior, our oldest brother, Dan, left to attend The College of the Holy Cross in Worcester, Massachusetts. Chris and I were so excited for our brother's independence, plus we thought we were so cool to have a brother in college! We packed up the Jeep Wagoneer so that it was stuffed from end to end like a sausage with Dan's belongings and drove the 3 to 4 hours to his new dorm. Once there, we helped tote bundles into his room until the car was empty and he was settled. It wasn't until my parents, Chris, and I returned to the car to head home without him that the first tear trickled down my cheek. Not only were we leaving Dan there, but in two more years, we would be doing this for Chris. I was devastated. In the back seat of the now empty Wagoneer, I leaned my wet cheek on Chris' shoulder and he put his arm around me. Although we didn't say anything, we both understood what was to come in the next few years.

In high school, I made the mistake of dating one of Chris' friends the summer before they went to college. Now it wasn't a mistake because the guy was an awful human being. It was a mistake because it was one of the 2 times I can remember that Chris was truly angry with me. Angry to the point that it lasted a while, and we went a few months speaking less and less. I remember thinking that he was simply jealous that his friend was choosing to spend time with me instead of him. But I also remember how upset I was that he was acting this way. We never came out and spoke about this time but once the relationship ended, it was as if it never happened.

Several months after his college graduation, Chris accepted a job at Kidder Peabody on Wall Street and later changed jobs to join the family of Cantor Fitzgerald. Chris loved his job with Cantor from the start and was quite successful. He realized that I had chosen a career that wasn't as lucrative, yet he never waved his monetary success in my face. Instead he found ways to let me enjoy it as well. When I needed extra money for a security deposit on an apartment, he was there to lend it to me, and he insisted I never pay it back. When I couldn't afford a moving company to help me move, he slept on the floor of my apartment, helped me carry bulky couches up mountainous stairwells, and took me out to dinner. One of my fondest memories was a spontaneous phone call I received.

I answered, "Hello?"

Chris asked, "Erin, what are you doing tonight?"

I responded, "Going out with some friends."

He insistently added, "You need to cancel. We're going to see the Lion King on Broadway."

I remember thinking that the show was sold out for months, yet Chris had gotten the tickets through one of his connections and had chosen to take me, his

Fairfield University graduation

The family at Mom and
Dad's 25th anniversary

Erin's wedding, October 6, 2000

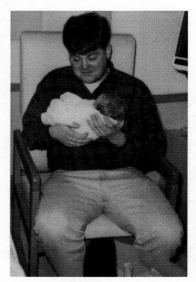

Chris holding his first nephew,
baby Conor (probably the first
time holding a newborn!)

Chris and Conor, Nantucket,
August, 2001 (the last
picture of Chris)

little sister. He could have taken anyone—a client, a girlfriend, his mother, but he chose to pick up the phone and call me. How special is that?!

For years, I had always called Chris to remind him of family birthdays, our parents' anniversary, and other various occasions in which he needed to call someone to wish them well. He had trouble remembering these special dates, yet he didn't have any trouble remembering my wedding day. My mother suggested strongly that he sleep at her house the night before the wedding to make sure he was in attendance and on time. It was a warm day in October and Chris was certainly feeling the heat, yet he put on his usual coy smile and looked dapper in his tux. At the end of the church ceremony, sweat was racing down most of the tuxedo clad men's backs, and we were all looking forward to processing out of the steamy church. As I approached the exit, I heard the sound of bagpipes and knew I hadn't arranged it. My new husband looked at me quizzically and I shrugged. Scanning the crowd, my eyes landed on Chris who was close to the piper. He caught my eye, gave me a nod and smile and I knew. The guy who had trouble remembering birthdays remembered my wedding day and arranged for the traditional sound of the bagpipes to celebrate this special day as a surprise.

It was the summer before that dark day in September and my family had taken our annual trip to Nantucket. Dan was there with his wife and two children, my parents, and Chris. It was the first year that I chose not to go. In years past, I had always found a way there, even though I couldn't take a week off work like the others. Several years I left my apartment in Westchester, NY at 4 a.m. on a Saturday, drove 4 hours to the ferry and returned late Sunday night only to go to work early Monday morning. One year, Mom and Dad paid for my flight so I wouldn't have to make the grueling drive and I would have more time to spend with the family on the beach. Yet, in 2001 I did not go. On Labor Day weekend, we all got together to celebrate Dan's birthday after they returned from Nantucket, and Chris let me know that it was NOT okay that I missed this trip. He didn't yell and he didn't make sarcastic comments in front of the family. He simply let me know in his quiet way, that this was something we didn't miss and I was wrong. This trip was about family and no matter what was going on in your life you found your way there. I remember leaving the party feeling disappointed in myself for the decision I made and him standing at the rolled down window of my car. My last words to him were, "I love you buddy." I cried to my husband of less than a year on my ride home that night because Chris was right. I don't think my husband understood how upset I was, but we agreed that we would go no matter what the following summer. Little did I know Chris would not be there the next summer or any summer thereafter.

September 11ᵗʰ 2001

Although I have detailed memories of our childhood, I do not remember much of that day. The beautiful, unblemished, bright blue sky of that morning is what I remember most. Since then, I cringe when I see such a clear sky and I search hopelessly for a single cloud. Chris did not own a cell phone and to be honest, I don't know that he would have called any of us if he did because he wouldn't have wanted us to worry. Ironically, Chris and I once had a conversation when I visited him at work and we had a drink at Windows on the World, about his emergency evacuation procedures which required them to go to the roof instead of down the stairs. What I remember most of that conversation is that he joked about how they would get all those people down from the roof, yet he didn't seem worried in the least. But that was the kind of guy he was. He never wanted you to worry about him and if he sensed worry or anguish, he turned it into a joke and made you relax with laughter. As I have said, I don't remember much from that day, but I would be lying if I said I don't think about what he experienced up there on the 104th floor inferno. I think about it everyday as well as many nights. What I do know for sure is that Chris Slattery left us with broken hearts, yet those broken hearts are filled with the incredible memories of a loving brother and devoted son. He will never, EVER be forgotten.

*   *   *

The above beautiful remembrance about Chris was written with many tears by my daughter, Erin.

Christopher was 31 years old on that tragic day; his life, like so many of the others lost, was just beginning. Chris was born in Brooklyn, New York and grew up on Long Island. He attended Chaminade High School and Fairfield University where he made lifelong friends. He worked for Cantor Fitzgerald for 7 years and as Erin mentioned, loved it. We have formed the Christopher Slattery Memorial Scholarship Foundation and are funding scholarships to both his high school and college in his name.

It is our family's hope that our country will never forget what happened that day and will continue to work to make sure that such a tragedy can never happen again.

By Linda Slattery

Daniel Afflitto

By Eleanor Afflitto,
Daniel's mother

On Sept. 11, 2001, terrorists took the lives of almost three thousand people and my son was one of them. Danny was a happy child, he was not one to sit back and watch others. Rather, he would join in any activity that was happening around him. He was happy, always with a huge grin; he got along just fine with his peers, family, teachers and coaches. He was loyal to both family and friends. Dan had a need for everything. He knew who he was and was most comfortable in that knowledge. But Dan was no saint, by any means. There are numbers of stories about him teasing his brother and enjoying every bit of his misbehavior.

In elementary school he would leave home often without his shoes, lunch, and homework, and come back home telling us that no one had reminded him to take these things. Dan wore glasses as a youngster and he often left them somewhere and we would hunt for them in the dark with a flashlight. On his way home from school he often stopped at friends of mine to visit for candy and cookies, never telling me where he was.

Danny grew up with a standard poodle named Pandora who was sure she was his mother. In junior high Danny flourished, making new friends, both good and bad, and needed to be reminded often that he was known by the company he kept. He was very outgoing, modeled in a fashion show and hosted a talent show, and managed to get himself into trouble often. One of his subjects in middle school was Home Economics. The project was to make an apron. Dan got an F in Home Economics. He did not like his apron and never submitted it to his teacher. He spent an hour making up a tall tale when he could have told the truth very easily.

One day in the middle of the winter he came home with one boot and one sock. When asked, "What happened to the other boot and sock?" He just looked down and shrugged his shoulders. Danny played soccer from the time he was a small child and he had a passion for the game and continued to play all through his school years.

High school was just one big party. He became Vice President of the student council, played varsity soccer and was always kind to underclassmen.

Danny playing soccer. He is the one in the middle.　　　Graduation from St Joe's

First Communion　　　Dan and his brother Joe

St. Joseph's University in Philadelphia was Danny's choice for college. He made life long friends. There are many who still keep in touch with me. He was President of the Crimson Key Society (a recruiting organization for the university), and was co-founder of St. Joe's first Fraternity, Sigma Phi Epsilon.

Danny went to Wall Street after college and thrived. One of his employers was a man named Eddie Mathews who was his mentor. Ed tells a story about Dan in a brand new Armani suit ready to go to meet clients. The pants were too long so Dan grabbed a stapler and shortened them.

He became the head equities trader, and ultimately, a partner at Cantor Fitzgerald and was employed by them on September 11.

He was married on May 1, 1999 to Stacey nee Rizzo and when he passed away he had a son Joseph-six months old and his wife was pregnant with Daniel Jr.

Not a day goes by when I do not think about him. I love you Danny!

Danny, Jr. High School, on right

Danny being Danny

Danny & President of St Joe's University

Danny in Jr. High as the Emcee

Dan & his brother Joe

Danny and Pandora

Dan & his good buddies

Dan on his wedding day

Danny's children,
Joseph & Daniel

Danny with wife Stacey

Kevin M. Prior

By Marian Prior,
Kevin's mother

Born with the heart and soul of a firefighter on January 18, 1973, Kevin knew at a very early age that be would be one of New York City's Bravest. In Bellmore, Long Island, where he lived his whole life, the sound of the fire horn would signal young Kevin to hop on his bike and rush down to the corner. Just two blocks from the nearest fire station, he could see the fire trucks race by on the main street around the corner. When he was old enough to take his bike off the block, he'd go to the fire station to watch the firefighters and the trucks turn out for a call. He was eleven years old when, on one of those races to the firehouse, he was hit by a car—not seriously hurt, but his bike was mangled.

Kevin was always a happy, easy-going kind of kid. He didn't clamor for extravagant birthday parties, but looked forward to homemade cake and celebrating with his two older brothers and cousins. He loved family gatherings. Whenever we gathered with family or friends and the hour grew late, Kevin would fall sound asleep in the middle of the floor. People could step over him, talk and laugh loudly, and he'd never be disturbed.

He loved camping trips and vacations at Lake George . . . always big fun with the cousins. Our family's introduction to camping included no amenities—no showers, no bathrooms, so only the heartiest could bear it for more than a night or two. But the hiking and the campfires made it great fun. Oh, but we did have an outhouse! And one night, Kevin's Dad took him for a middle of the night visit. Dad carried barefoot Kevin while Kevin held the battery-powered light. I could hear Dad's steps as he carried Kevin there . . . crunch, crunch, crunch on the bluestone pebbles . . . then the door of the outhouse went *SLAM!* In a little while I heard the door slam again, and crunch, crunch, crunch again along the bluestone. Then Kevin and his father appeared in the tent, but without the light! It was just too much for Dad to handle the boy and the light too. So, better it was the light that was dropped down you-know-where. The next morning, Uncle Mike made his visit to the outhouse and returned with the light! No one wanted to hear about how he got it out of you-know-where!

FF. KEVIN M. PRIOR
FDNY Squad 252
LT. Bellmore FD

As a boy, Kevin played with Matchbox cars with his friend from next door for hours on end, and he collected Smurfs (little blue elf-like plastic characters in every costume imaginable). He liked an "Emergency!" board game—not that it was such a great game, but he loved to push the emergency vehicles around the board making the screaming sound of the siren.

He attended the local Catholic grammar school of Saint Barnabas the Apostle through the eighth grade. He was a cub scout and an average student;

he was a shepherd in the Christmas pageant. Always a willing helper, he raised the American flag in the school yard, and didn't know that his younger cousin proudly watched from inside his classroom and told his friends, "That's my cousin raising the flag." At home, Kevin would bring in the garbage cans when he could barely lift them, and he mowed the lawn for his father before he was even a teenager. Kevin was never a star athlete, but he had fun playing basketball and running track for CYO. He could be a bit clumsy, sometimes in too much of a hurry for his legs to keep up. He might just fall off the stoop while waiting for me to open the door. On a hot August afternoon, while showing off for his cousin Teresa, he was walking around the rim of the above-ground pool in our backyard when he fell off and broke his arm. He was seven years old, but he knew it was serious. His arm was misshapen at the break and he came running into the house screaming: "I broke my arm! Get me to the hospital quick!"

By the time he was fourteen, he had a scanner in his room and monitored local fire calls day and night. He knew all the codes; he could tell you which fire trucks were responding to what kind of call. He'd listen until he heard the code to indicate the job was done and the trucks were on the way back to the fire station. He joined the Junior Firematic Squad, and the local firehouse became the place he loved to be. By now he had a motorized scooter, which made doing his paper route a breeze, and also provided easy transport to the firehouse. He'd hang out there whenever they would let him; cleaning the trucks, sweeping the floor, helping out at special events. Kevin would do anything for the Bellmore Volunteer Fire Department. He was so proud, as Captain of the Junior Firematic Squad, when they won first place in a Firefighters' Parade. Memorial Day was always a special occasion for us. Kevin would, of course, be involved in the Bellmore parade with the Volunteer Fire Department, and he'd be anxious for us to see him march with the fire department. So, we'd go out for the parade, and then we'd go to the firehouse for hotdogs. And traditionally, that would be the day that we planted our vegetable garden, while Kevin stayed at the firehouse until the crowds were gone and he helped with the cleanup.

Whenever a senior firefighter paid any attention to him, Kevin was thrilled. Later, as a regular firefighter himself, he remembered how special he felt as a Junior when an older firefighter took the time to show him equipment or describe procedure. Kevin was happy to do the same for the Juniors that came after him.

Kevin loved his dog, Pal. Originally the puppy was promised to his older brother Gerard as soon as he was old enough to be responsible for taking care of a dog. When Gerard joined the Marine Corps, Pal became Kevin's special buddy. He taught Pal tricks and let her sleep at the foot of his bed. Eventually, Pal came to the end of her years and we knew it was time to put her to sleep, but she beat us to it. Kevin came home from school to find Pal seemingly asleep at the foot of his bed. Kevin kept Pal's red collar in his desk drawer forever after that.

He attended Holy Trinity Diocesan High School from 1987 to 1991. He loved his high school years—he said he had the best time. He went out for Freshman Football, which only lasted long enough to get a picture of him suited up! He was a better spectator than participant. I remember how excited he was about his first car, a red Mustang, which he was probably too inexperienced to handle. Cruising down to the beach with his friends one afternoon, he lost control on the parkway and had an accident which totaled the car. Luckily, he and a friend only suffered minor injuries. When I saw Kevin in the hospital getting stitches over his eye, he admitted tearfully, "I screwed up." He did become a better driver. Years later, when he took chauffeur training with the FDNY to drive the fire engine, he achieved a perfect score. He worked part-time as a busboy for the local steakhouse, and he dated one special girl in high school. They remained friends long after they had gone their separate ways.

The criminal justice courses he took over three years at Long Island University, C. W. Post campus, prepared him for the year and a half he would spend as a New York City Police Officer. A clever fellow, Kevin quickly figured out that summer sessions were shorter and you earned the same amount of credit. Kevin was proud to follow in the footsteps of his father who was a police officer for twenty years. Although he could have requested to serve under his father's badge number, he declined to ask for it when he leaned that it had already been assigned to someone else. He didn't want to take the badge from another officer when it was always Kevin's intention to transfer to the FDNY. He hoped it wouldn't be long before they would call him.

Kevin received a perfect score on the test for the FDNY and aced the physical and performance tests. When he knew that he would be in the next Fire Academy class, he brought home champagne and we celebrated. Kevin would have the career he always dreamed of . . . the best job in the world, the only job he ever wanted. It was July 1995.

During the next three years Kevin settled into firehouse life, gained experience, and was always eager to do more. He loved the camaraderie, and the firehouse humor which included practical jokes and teasing each other. He learned to cook, eagerly taking his turn in the firehouse kitchen. Firefighters share a special bond that makes them "brothers" to each other and Kevin loved this "brotherhood." His dedication and enthusiasm on the job was obvious to his supervisors. He always wanted to be where the action was. And so, in July of 1998, Kevin became a charter member of Special Operations Squad 252. He couldn't have been happier, as he looked forward to advanced training and the big jobs he would go to. He told me, "If I die tomorrow, I die a happy man."

He always looked forward to going to work. Frequently, he worked on holidays so the firefighters with families could be home with their kids. He said that when he had a family of his own, the younger guys would work for him on holidays. But he always managed to be off on the night of the Bellmore Volunteer Fire Department's Santa Runs . . . the big rig would glow with holiday decorations and lights, and the siren would signal that "Santa" and his fire department helpers were riding through the neighborhood, visiting children, hopefully before they fell asleep.

Cheerfully optimistic, he loved to say, "Don't sweat the small stuff." There was a Ziggy cartoon that Kevin kept on his desk that said, "If you sweat the small stuff, you just end up with a pile of soggy stuff." Occasionally, preoccupied with what was going on in his own life, he would act in a thoughtless way. I'd confront him and let him know that I was disappointed. He'd try to defend his actions, and an argument at that moment wouldn't resolve anything. So I'd write him a letter about it. I wouldn't hear any more about it for a day or so, and then he would come to me and say that he understood my feelings. He had a good sense of what was really important in life. During a stressful day, he was quick to take note of worse things that were happening to other people. Then he'd say, "And I thought I was having a bad day!" If frustration got in the way of doing anything, he'd patiently say, "We'll figure it out." I remember he often said, "Keep it simple . . ." and that reminds me that life need not be as complicated as we sometimes make it.

Kevin was proud of his Irish heritage. After thinking about it for a year or two, he finally got to visit Ireland, the homeland of his grandparents, in the summer of 2001. Being where his grandfather grew up meant a lot to him, and he came home with great stories of the fun he had with his Irish relatives. St. Patrick's Day was one of his favorite holidays. He'd go to Mass in the morning and then take the train into the city to march with the NYC Fire Department in the St. Patrick's Day Parade.

In 2001 Kevin's life was exactly as he wanted it to be. He loved his job, had many friends, and was looking forward to the rest of his life. He was engaged to be married, and he hoped to one day have his own home and family and a dog. He expected to advance in his career with the FDNY. He was already studying for promotion to Lieutenant. But on that beautiful Tuesday morning, September 11th, 2001, out of the clearest blue sky, evil gripped New York City when terrorists hijacked airplanes and crashed them into the Twin Towers of the World Trade Center. Lives were changed forever. Dreams died, and ordinary people became heroes, Kevin among them.

He was working that morning when the call came in. He responded with five other members of Squad 252. The last that was heard of him was that he was on his way up the staircase of the North Tower answering a call for help from other firefighters. No one from Squad 252 made it out of the North Tower before it collapsed.

At the age of 28, Kevin died doing the job he loved. I'll never know how many people were saved that day because of him. But I know that in his short life, he left us wonderful memories of the time we had together. His optimism and enthusiasm are an example for living, which encourages me every day. Kevin is greatly missed, but knowing him has been the greatest blessing.

Dave J. Fontana

By Toni Fontana,
David's mother

Dave with Aidan

Lifeguards – Dave 3rd from right

Dave (top) with brother Ed.

"Do you know Dave Fontana? I love Dave Fontana." Aidan was five years old and had just started kindergarten when his father, Lt. David J. Fontana, FDNY, was killed fighting the fire at the World Trade Center on September 11th, 2001.

Dave and Aidan   Dave

September 2001

Dave was well known in Park Slope, the Brooklyn neighborhood where he lived and where his Squad 1 firehouse was located. He and Aidan often walked to the nearby stores to buy toys and books and ice cream, Aidan riding on Dave's shoulders. Dave walked Aidan to school, and in Prospect Park, a few blocks away, he taught him to ride his bike. Dave had collections of Star Wars toys, Thomas the Tank Engine train sets, and Revolutionary War hats and stories. He took Aidan to Williamsburg, Virginia to show him where the stories happened.

Dave grew up the second youngest of seven children. With four brothers, he had his share of adventures. On summer vacations, he and his family went camping from Maine to Key West, and visited places like Valley Forge and St. Augustine, which helped nurture his interests in nature and history.

He loved to swim and was on the swim team at his high school. In college he played rugby with great enthusiasm. At home, he and his friend Andy ran together to keep in shape. When it was time to go, Andy would appear at the back door whistling bird calls.

David Fontana was a man with a love for people and a great sense of humor. During high school and college he worked as an ocean lifeguard at Jones Beach and Fire Island. While off duty from protecting the swimmers from wild waves and big crowds, he built up his strength and skills by rowing surf boats with another lifeguard. On their days off, they rowed against other lifeguards in races at Sag Harbor, Long Island, Newport, Rhode Island, and in New York Harbor at South Street Seaport. In the lifeguard shack during thunderstorms, he entertained the other guards. Using the markers he found in the shack, Dave drew faces on the bottoms of his toes and performed plays with his Toe-Puppet Theater.

Dave's artistic talent was developed at C.W. Post College, where he graduated with a degree in sculpture. Some of his works were eight foot high star-shaped towers of steel. At the beach, he carved logs into a seven foot high Kahuna (a totem with its tongue sticking out) to guarantee good waves for surfing, and a six-foot tall monkey to make people smile. For his firehouses, he carved wooden life-sized statues of a bunker-clad fireman, and St. Florian, the patron saint of firefighters

When Dave graduated FDNY probationary school at Randall's Island, he was one of the probies assigned to display their skills. His challenge was to rappel down the outside of a six story building. His mother was more worried than impressed. After the ceremony, they celebrated with lunch at a little restaurant on 93rd Street. Going in and sitting at a table by the window, his mother looked out and saw Fireman Dave peering out from behind a tree and smiling impishly like a little boy, to tell her nothing had changed, not to worry!

Dave loved America and its history. During World War II, his uncle Ed was killed at Bastogne in the Battle of the Bulge. Dave went to Europe to visit the military cemetery in Luxembourg where Sgt. Eduardo Fontana is buried. Later, while working at Ladder 122, Dave became curious about the firefighters from his house who had been killed in World War II and wanted to know more about them. This research expanded to include all the firefighters who had died in the war. While doing his research, he helped organize the data at the George Mand Library at the FDNY site on Randall's Island. With the information he found, he helped put up a memorial for those men at his firehouse. Today the FDNY has used his research to install a permanent memorial at their training center on Randall's Island, with a Fire Department helmet for each soldier who died in World War II and Iraq, and a book of their biographies for visitors to read which their families can add to and sign.

In Brooklyn, where Dave lived, the church of St. Francis Xavier was six blocks from his apartment. On a lovely summer day in 1996, Dave, walking with his family, carried Aidan in his arms to the church for his baptism. His face, wreathed in smiles, made everyone else smile.

Dave with Aidan at Christmas time

Dave and Aidan (April 2001)

Dave and nephew Rich

Jones Beach Long Island N.Y

Ireland 2000

As Aidan grew bigger, he loved to wrestle with Dave. One day they were having their usual fun when four-year-old Aidan was bumped and started to cry. When his wife Marian asked what had happened, Dave said, "He started it!" Everyone laughed.

In 1986 and 1987, Dave got to visit Ireland and finally meet his Irish cousins. In 1988, he went back again with his mother and sister. On these trips and others, he grew to love both Ireland and his family there. In Glengoole, County Tipperary, where his great-grandmother had been born, there is a plaque in the parish church that says:

In loving memory of
    Lieut. David J. Fontana F.D.N.Y
    Squad 1 Brooklyn
    who gave his life saving others
    at the World Trade Center
    Sept. 11, 2001
    "Greater love than this no man hath."
    Great-grandson of Ellen Norton
    of Glengoole, Co. Tipperary
    He loved his family, Glengoole, and Ireland.

In remembering Dave at his memorial service, a woman his mother's age came up to her and told her how she missed his smile and hug as she walked by the firehouse. His love reached out to many people. He is greatly missed, but also happily remembered. In September 2001, his mother wrote this poem:

Dave loved to walk up the hill in Glengoole
To see the stars,
To taste a pint in the local pub,
To go to the beach to feel the sun and waves,
To pull the oars in an open boat,
To swim in the ponds on Cape Cod,
To go to little islands in Maine,
To fly in a helicopter over Hawaiian volcanoes,
To walk in a Virginia marsh to look at the wild ponies,
To hear the laughing gulls call,
To see the moon race behind the city buildings,
To carry Aidan on his shoulders.

When you are out on a starry night
Or on a windy beach
Or in a salt marsh in gentle rain
Or on a city street
And see a man with a little boy on his shoulders,
Think of Dave. He'll be there.
He lives in our hearts and memories.

Captain Vincent F. Giammona

By Dorothy Giammona,
Vincent's mother

Vinny, 3 years old, 1964

Vinny's First Holy Communion, 1968
Front: Linda and Vinny
Back: Louise and Mom

Vinny Giammona,
1st Grade Picture, 1966

Just one big happy family, 1969
Left to Right: Vinny, Louise, Linda, Steven with Mom

Another Sunday watching Vinny Race, 1970
Louise, Mom (in back)
Linda, Steven, Vinny (in front)

Vinny Giammona,
High School Graduation.
St. Francis High School, 1979

The Exclusive "Eagles" Track
Team, 1971. Vinny and Dad

Giammona kids, 1972
In front: Linda and Steven
In back: Louise and Vinny

Elementary School Graduation, 1975.
St. Kevin's School. Vinny and Dad

Captain Vincent F. Giammona was born on September 11, 1961. He was named after his father and followed his footsteps into the Fire Department but liked to be called "Vinny G." From childhood to adulthood Vinny loved, laughed, and lived everyday to its fullest. As his parents we remember fondly some lessons he learned as a young child that made him so special.

When Vinny was in kindergarten his teacher asked that we practice skipping at home and help him develop this skill. Happily, every night his big sister would skip with him around the dining room table, again and again. It wasn't an easy task, but Vinny finally caught on adding his own style.

He also was a young entrepreneur. He wanted to sell flower seeds to raise money for his fourth grade class. With his younger sister tagging along, he went to all our neighbors and convinced them to buy flower seeds. He was proud of his accomplishment and his sister was hungry from all the work—so he treated her to lunch with the flower seed money! That day he learned you cannot spend other people's money—even if that means saying "no" to your sister! This was a difficult lesson for a very protective brother.

After his younger brother was born, Vinny had another reason to test our parenting skills. Since his younger brother was the only family member with blonde hair, Vinny often teased him by telling him he was adopted. Naturally, this teasing stopped as soon as he realized his younger brother wasn't laughing and truly believed what he was told. Vinny learned that a big brother's words were just as important as his actions.

At his elementary school, Vinny "acted up" during lunch and was suspended from eating lunch at school for a couple of days. Known as the "original spin doctor," he told me that he just missed me and wanted to ride his bike home and have lunch. As his mother, I felt his tell-tale grin was priceless but knew it meant trouble!

When he was twelve, like all kids his age, he was convinced he was cool and he did things that most kids do. One day he decided to call my husband and me by our first names, but that did not last too long. Vinny quickly realized how blessed he was to have parents and a family who spent time with him. He also grew tired of being called by his full name—Vincent Francis Giammona—every time his friends were around!

It was clear Vinny was growing up and loving every minute of it. By the time he started high school he decided he needed his own space and moved downstairs to our unfinished (no frills) basement. He took his bed and told his younger brother, "Now we both have our own rooms!" Somehow it seemed to make sense.

Another thing that always made sense throughout his childhood and adulthood was running track. Vinny loved to run. He ran for St Kevin's Elementary School and for St. Francis Prep High School. However, he was most happy when he ran

Fire Fighter Vinny Giammona,
special training at "The Rock", August 2001

Lt. Vincent Francis Giammona,

Vinny Giammona on the job.
"All work. No play."

Vinny Pull Box Pub
Dad, Mom, Vinny

Father and Son.
Captain Vincent
Michael Giammona
and Lt. Vincent
Francis Giammona
"Couldn't Be
Prouder"

113

by his father's side. Vinny and his father ran with the very exclusive track team, "The Eagles," which consisted of just the two of them. They would happily run 8 to 10 miles to Woodside from Bayside just for lunch with Nonnie (grandma).

He became Captain of his freshman track team and he loved being part of the team, win or lose. The final track meet of the year was the big race for Vinny because that was where the top runners from public and private school competed. Typically, the same runners on each side placed at every previous race, so Vinny knew who his competition was and was prepared to run his best. Although my son came in second that day, he knew the importance of being a good sport and went over to shake the hand of the winner. Unfortunately, the winner refused to shake Vinny's hand. With disappointment, that boy's father told him that the "true winner" lost the race. That boy grew up and now tells his children of the lesson he learned from "Vinny G.", which is how someone can still achieve great things just by doing their best.

By senior year, Vinny was not interested in a school ring or going to his senior prom. All he wanted was to be a New York City Firefighter, just like his father. He went to college and worked hard with the anticipation of fulfilling his dream. In 1982, he was called to the FDNY and he could not have been happier and my husband and I could not have been prouder.

We miss our son Vinny each and every day but we are grateful for the lessons, laughs, and the love that he shared.

*   *   *

Remembering my big brother Vinny

Looking through family photo albums, one would find some unflattering pictures of me, where it is obvious that diet and exercise were not as important as they are to me today. So you can imagine how difficult it was growing up in the 70's with Farrah Fawcett posters everywhere and having an older brother who was born with the metabolism of a gazelle. Since Vinny never had to struggle with his weight, he was never quite as sensitive as you would hope an older and more understanding brother would be of his younger and "huskier" sister. And so between the Casper and the Brady Bunch years, Vinny loved to torment me. He built clubhouses with the other bad boys of Bayside and they dismembered many of my Scott Baio dolls. The evidence was there even then; he was a leader, bringing out the truly best qualities in any pre-teen.

But one day, I don't know exactly when, my big brother looked at me a little differently. Maybe it was because I stopped arm wrestling him for Twinkees, but there came a time when he allowed me to tag along without our mother forcing him, and let me hang out with his really "cool" friends. I became his student and

Giammona Trip to Hawaii 1982
Left to Right: Dad, Mom,
Linda, Vinny, Steven

Vinny Giammona.
"Off Duty" 1984

On top of the world.
Vinny after he "got
on the job", 1984/5

Vinny Giammona (FF) 1985
"Just happy to be here"

FF Vinvent Giammona (center)
with two fire fighters
Ladder 136 (Fellow FFs)

he my teacher. Wide-eyed and willing to hear what my big brother had to say, I became his greatest fan. Vinny showed me the way—he took me to my first Ramones concert at Central Park, he taught me and all my really cute girlfriends how to drive in my parent's 1972 Ventura. He showed me around the Village and introduced me to McSorley's. Naturally, with all this attention, access to fake ID's, and free rides to anywhere in the tri—state area, all of my girlfriends fell in love with Vinny. How could they not? He was 17, had his own room in the basement, had an Oldsmobile Cutlass, and he was fearless. He had the confidence of an Olympian and a heart of gold. And he knew there was only one thing he was meant to be . . . and that was a New York City Firefighter.

Once he got the badge, there was no stopping him. He didn't walk, he sauntered. He didn't smile, he beamed. He didn't enter a room, he absorbed it. He truly was 10 feet tall. And now he was on "The Job". He had the brotherhood—the pride—the badge—the honor—and the privilege to learn what so few had the courage to know and experience. For Vinny, it was a calling to become a New York City Firefighter. And no one knew it better than him.

Of course he took full advantage of the job's perks. You know—free parking, free admission, free beer, pretty girls and the mother-load of all civil servant perks, the "Power of the Badge!" I must admit however, I had some selfish motives in mind when Vinny was going through his FDNY training. But before I could say, "Proby Party," Vinny tagged me as his little sister and threatened anyone who even looked in my direction. For years I was introduced with "This is my sister Linda—you touch her, and I'll kill you". Naturally, I developed a crush on every firefighter I was told NOT to speak to, and there lay the bane of my existence.

Over the years my big brother taught me many things. But the things that mean the most are the ones that he held closest to his heart. To Vinny, family was the most important thing in life. He believed we should be good to one another and take care of each other. Honor your mother and listen to your father. Respect your heritage, while building your future. Laugh as much as possible, and never say "never." Make a difference each day, and don't wait for the big moment. I think the reason why so many people were drawn to Vinny was because he was the "real deal". He lived what he believed. His actions spoke louder than his words. Vinny didn't have to say, "I love being a father" because you saw it when he took his girls to the Home Depot. You didn't need to hear him say, "I enjoy hanging out with my friends" because you knew he gave a whole new meaning to backyard barbecue. And anyone who knew anything about Vinny understood that he personified the term "New York City's Bravest." I can say after meeting with so many firefighters over the last few years, that although I have lost my big brother, I have gained 10,000, and Vinny is in each and every one of them. I also see Vinny in my father's eyes and near my mother's heart. I hear him in my daughter's laughter and feel him through my husband's strength. I recognize

Vinny's steady hand in my younger brother's guidance, and honor in my sister's fortitude. I see Vinny in every firefighter, police officer, and military personnel I meet, and understand his actions better each time the nation sings "God Bless America". My big brother is not lost, he is everywhere I go. And every time I see a truck thunder by and hear the sirens sound, I hold him that much closer to my heart.

By Linda Giammona Julian, sister

Joseph Hunter

By Tessie Hunter,
Joseph's mother

Firefighter Joseph Hunter, FDNY Squad 288, was born on September 29, 1969 to parents Joseph and Tessie Hunter in Brooklyn, New York. Joseph was the third child for Joe and Tessie, and the first brother to sisters Margaret and Teresa. Finally, a son! His family moved from Brooklyn to South Hempstead on Long Island, New York when Joe was a baby. Just a few years later, Joe received a brother of his own when Sean was born. There was no prouder family!

Joseph had an infectious smile from the beginning. A beautiful, handsome son, he was "all boy." Joseph was a great baby, who loved people and fun. Joe was also the serious type. Although he was private, he displayed traits of being very caring, honest, sensitive, responsible, modest, bright, and quick-witted.

Joe was very active in sports. He played baseball, ice hockey, roller hockey, and he loved skiing and riding his bicycle. He loved anything to do with the outdoors. Joseph's greatest punishment would be being kept indoors for any length of time.

During his four years of high school, Joe played football with the Cyclones at South Side High School in Rockville Centre. Joe was a New York Mets baseball fan, a New York Giants football fan, and a New York Islander hockey fan.

Joe showed early signs of his fascination with the Fire Department. Joe began to notice the fire siren that went off daily at 6:00pm. At the early age of four, Joe

Joseph—Baldwin Bombers football, age 12

would race his Big Wheel to the corner of his block in hopes of catching a glimpse of the shiny red fire truck on the move with its screaming sirens. As Joe grew older, he would follow the trucks as far as he was allowed to go by bicycle.

When Joe turned 10, a new family moved into the neighborhood. Lucky for Joe, the family had a son. That son, Matt, became Joe's best friend. Even better, Matt's father was a firefighter! Not only was Matt's father a firefighter, he was a valued member of the drill team for a local fire department. The drill team is a team of volunteer firefighters who race and compete against other volunteer fire departments in different events, using firefighting race trucks and other fire fighting equipment. The races were held every Saturday from Memorial Day to Labor Day. Joe and Matt made it to most of those tournaments, year after year.

At the age of 11, Joe had his own drill team practicing in his driveway and backyard. A group of Joe's neighborhood buddies, along with a little red wagon, Dad's ladder, a garden hose, and the shed were used to recreate the action of the racing tournaments.

When Joe turned 18, he was old enough to join the South Hempstead Fire Department as a volunteer. Now it was Joe's turn to fulfill his dream and to race with the drill team. Joe did so for 13 years as the hydrant man for the South Hempstead Rascals. Joe's dedication to this passion was incredible. Joe has been referred to as the best hydrant man in Nassau County by many, which meant he could jump off of the race truck, get the hose attachment on the fire hydrant and

On graduation from Fire Academy

turn on the water in fractions of a second. Many other drill teams tried to recruit Joe, but his devotion was to South Hempstead's team.

Through the years, Joe was somewhat of a fixture in the firehouse. If he wasn't tending to the normal firehouse duties, he was often found reading or studying in the conference room of the firehouse. Joe could easily be goofing around with the guys in the firehouse, but when the siren went off, Joe became a "man of action". He was serious about firefighting and liked discussing fire training.

Joe graduated form Hofstra University in 1994, where he earned a Bachelors of Science in Business Management. While attending Hofstra, Joe took the written exam for the New York City Fire Department. Joe knew exactly what he wanted to do with his life. Joe wanted to be a New York City Firefighter. He referred to his dream as "my baby." Joe entered the Academy in October 1995 and graduated January 16, 1996.

In 1999, Joe was handpicked to join Squad 288 in Maspeth, Queens. Members of the squad receive specialized training in areas like confined space rescue, collapse rescue and terrorism. Joe was referred to by another Squad 288 firefighter as being "the sharpest guy I have ever worked with". There is brotherhood amongst firemen like no other. These men and women have complete faith in and complete respect for each other.

Joseph Hunter, Squad 288

Firefighter Joseph Hunter, FDNY, lost his life at the World Trade Center, on September 11th, 2001. Joe died because of intolerance and hatred, in an act of terrorism. Joseph was not known by the evil people that wished to harm Americans that day; Joseph was a beloved son, an adored loving brother, a proud uncle, a brother in law, a proud Irish American, a cousin, a nephew, a confidant and a friend. Joe saved countless lives that day. Now he is a hero.

Thank you Joe, for your heroism!

Steven Coakley

By Carol and Vincent Coakley,
Vincent's parents

Steven brought happiness to our lives on October 25, 1964. He was born at Good Samaritan Hospital in West Islip, New York. He weighed 8lbs 8oz and was very healthy. For his first birthday his grandfather, Michael Teodorowicz, a New York City Firefighter, bought him a rideable fire truck and child's helmet.

Steven's 26' Bertram Boat

A37

AMERICA'S ORDEAL

A Fisherman Who Became a Hero

By Kathryn Wellin
STAFF WRITER

Teach a boy to fish, and he will stay out of trouble, goes the adage. And so Vinny Coakley started his boy, Steven, fishing on the Great South Bay and the Atlantic Ocean every Saturday and Sunday.

When Steven was 4, he caught his first freshwater fish. On his 15th birthday, he nabbed a 140-pound dusky shark and eight tunas in the 30-pound class. The shark's jaws, yellow and ossified, grimace from the kitchen wall in his parents' Deer Park home, where Steven, a firefighter with Ladder 217 in Bedford-Stuyvesant, also lived. Coakley has been missing since Sept. 11.

Reminders of his life hang on the Coakleys' walls — eight plaques in eight years for bravery as a Wyandanch volunteer firefighter, a diploma from the New York City Fire Academy, pictures of Coakley and his nieces.

For Coakley's first birthday, his grandfather Michael Teodorowicz, a New York City firefighter, bought him a ridable toy fire truck and a child's helmet. Coakley never expressed aloud an interest in firefighting, but at 17, three years after his grandfather died, he joined the Wyandanch fire volunteers, his mother, Carol, said.

Thursday would have been Coakley's 37th birthday. He was four years away from retiring permanently to the Madeira Bay, Fla., home he had transformed from a bungalow to a two-story palace with the help of his sister, Kara Walker, of Charlotte, N.C., an architect.

About eight years ago, he saw the house on his way to a Giants away game and knew he had found home. The day he bought the house was the happiest day of his life, his father said, as he showed a picture of his son smiling in his car on the way to sign the deed.

"This is his backyard," his father said,

pointing to a picture of the Boca Ciega Bay.

In that backyard was a 1965 Bertram fishing boat that Coakley meticulously restored for boating outings with his girlfriend, Linda New, and friends John and Julie Kauzlarich at Shell Island. Relaxing with friends on his boat was his passion after years spent on the water, but fishing also taught him how to be helpful.

Around the firehouse Coakley was known as MacGyver, after the character in the old TV series, because he could and would fix anything needing retooling at the station. He would trade shifts with his firehouse buddies, stringing together vacation time to spend in Florida. Every year, however, he dragged his friends down south with him for a golf fund-raiser in memory of Ashley Nielsen, the 4-year-old daughter of a colleague's cousin. Through this effort, Coakley met David Moore, a tight end with the NFL's

Tampa Bay Buccaneers and part of Nielsen's extended family. The two had been fishing mates ever since.

Whether he was driving 36 straight hours to Charleston, S.C., with a generator truck to help the Hurricane Hugo relief efforts, or earning the 1987 Wyandanch Volunteer Fireman of the Year Award for saving a trapped woman who was critically burned, Coakley always said, "No big deal."

"Mom and Dad say, 'Big deal,'" his father said as he paged through albums filled with photos and lures. "Teach a boy to fish, and he will become a hero," his father said.

Visitation will be Friday from 2 to 4 and 7 to 9 p.m. at the Boyd-Caratozzolo Funeral Home in Deer Park. A memorial service is scheduled for 10:15 a.m. Saturday at St. Cyril & Methodius Church in Deer Park.

Firefighter Steven Coakley in uniform and at right above with fishing buddy David Moore of the Tampa Bay Buccaneers

As days and weeks went by, he learned how to ride a tricycle, balance himself on a pony ride, fly kites at the beach, and try to swim with Dad's help. He was very active in soccer and baseball, plus every two weeks he went fishing with his dad and sister Kara. For his 15th birthday, his dad charted a fishing boat and they fished all day. By 4 P.M. Steve caught a 140 lb dusky shark plus 8 tunas. We had the jaw and teeth preserved by taxidermy; the mounted jaw is in his Florida house.

As for future years, Steven loved to enter all contests. For example, for Halloween he was a female nurse, went skiing and had to hop on a mechanical horse down the hill. He made a cardboard boat around his waist and dressed as the captain of a ship etc. He always won 1st prize. Steve's Dad's hobby was restoring old boats and 1940 cars. They both put many hours of labor with great results. After high school, he worked for Magee Oil Company and then 4 years at the

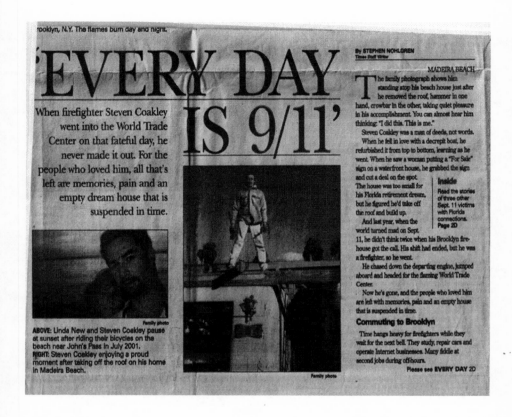

rooklyn, N.Y. The flames burn day and night.

'EVERY DAY IS 9/11'

When firefighter Steven Coakley went into the World Trade Center on that fateful day, he never made it out. For the people who loved him, all that's left are memories, pain and an empty dream house that is suspended in time.

By STEPHEN NOHLGREN
Times Staff Writer

MADEIRA BEACH

The family photograph shows him standing atop his beach house just after he removed the roof, hammer in one hand, crowbar in the other, taking quiet pleasure in his accomplishment. You can almost hear him thinking: "I did this. This is me."

Steven Coakley was a man of deeds, not words. When he fell in love with a decrepit boat, he refurbished it from top to bottom, learning as he went. When he saw a woman putting a "For Sale" sign on a waterfront house, he grabbed the sign and cut a deal on the spot.

The house was too small for his Florida retirement dream, but he figured he'd take off the roof and build up.

And last year, when the world turned mad on Sept. 11, he didn't think twice when his Brooklyn firehouse got the call. His shift had ended, but he was a firefighter, so he went.

He chased down the departing engine, jumped aboard and headed for the flaming World Trade Center.

Now he's gone, and the people who loved him are left with memories, pain and an empty house that is suspended in time.

Inside
Read the stories of three other Sept. 11 victims with Florida connections. Page 2D

Commuting to Brooklyn

Time hangs heavy for firefighters while they wait for the next bell. They study, repair cars and operate Internet businesses. Many fiddle at second jobs during offhours.

Please see EVERY DAY 2D

ABOVE: Linda New and Steven Coakley pause at sunset after riding their bicycles on the beach near John's Pass in July 2001.
RIGHT: Steven Coakley enjoying a proud moment after taking off the roof on his home in Madeira Beach.

Family photo
Family photo

Town of Babylon as a tree trimmer. During this time, Steven joined Wyandanch volunteer Fire Department. January 1987, F.F. Steven and Lt. Brian Dunleavy found an unconscious woman in a burning house. She had burns on 40% of her body and lung damage and was transported to Good Samaritan Hospital. Steven Coakley had burns on his neck and Lt. Dunleavy had heat exhaustion. Steven has eight plaques on his parents' living room wall. His most special was one for Fireman of the year 1987. On August 15th 1990, Steven became a New York City Firefighter. He graduated from the academy on October 18, 1990. Steven was assigned to Engine 217 on De Kalb Avenue in Brooklyn New York and remained there until 9/11/01.

During that time Steven bought a house on water front property and a 25' Bertram boat in Florida. It was his dream to retire there. He would trade shifts with his pals, do double shifts and fly firefighters and their wives to Maderie Beach to give them a vacation. Today his beloved Kara has them fly into Tampa.

The firefighters and their families are bused to a hotel. They have a busy weekend schedule which includes golfing, boating, tail gating at Tampa to see the Buccaneers play and a special party at night clubs. This continues to be done to "Never Forget" the people of 9/11. Some of Steven's favorite sayings were: "Can I help you?" "No big deal." and "Work hard, play hard."

Steven was always helping others:

When he was at Wyandanch Fire House, he and another FF drove 36 hours straight to Charleston, S.C. with a generator truck to help "Hurricane Hugo" relief.

Once a month, on Steven's day off, he would drive an 18-wheeler of carnival equipment for shows starting February to September. He loved helping out.

At Engine 217, Steven was known as "McGyver," the character on TV series because he could and would fix anything needing retooling at the station.

Every year, he would ask and take friends to his Florida house for a golf fund-raising in Memory of a 4 year old girl of a colleague's cousin.

Steven was a special person. He was dearly loved and he is greatly missed. He lived his life to the fullest.

A friend and a hero

Re: *Fun-loving New York firefighter, so at home at beach, is missing,* about firefighter Steve Coakley, Sept. 20.

As I sit at my computer, Steve's girlfriend, Linda, and my wife are waiting the necessary three or four hours in a New York airport to fly home after spending three days with the firefighters of Engine 217—with much of their time seeking closure with Steve's parents.

Steve was my best friend, and a bit different than one might think after reading Amy Wimmer's article. I would like for your readers to know the real Steve, the Steve that my daughter loves because, "He always listened to me." (A real compliment from an 11-year-old!) The Steve that, with a fractured foot, sprinted the length of Shell Island to get help for a young man who was having a seizure. The Steve, who first came to Pinellas County to take part in a charity golf tournament for the daughter of one of his retired firefighter brothers. The Steve who was the first one to reach for his billfold and sometimes the only one to make sure everybody got home safe.

Steven and Dr. John of the
"Buccaners."

age 9, October 13,
4ᵗʰ Grade

age 2, with Grandma
and Grandpa Teodorowicz

Sept. 16, '72,
John and Steven,
Soccer Game

Steven and his
sister Kara Coakley

Steven likes to look at books—
going to be President—age 2?

January 26, 1987/Fire News/Page 29

HEROIC ACTION SAVES TRAPPED WOMAN IN WYANDANCH

A Wyandanch woman is alive after being rescued from her blazing house by firefighters, who had to fight their way into the house with a charged handline, past a wall of flame, to get to the woman.

The Wyandanch Fire Co. received an alarm for a house fire on the afternoon of January 15, shortly after 1600 hours at 11 Jamaica Avenue. First on the scene was Ex-Chief Jim Brown, a Town of Babylon Fire Coordinator (1-0-2), who called the dispatcher to advise responding units that it was a working fire and there was an occupant trapped within.

A man, woman and their young daughter and granddaughter were in the house when the fire started on the ground floor. They all got out

woman who was on the second floor and was overcome by smoke and heat. First Lt. Brian Dunleavy and firefighter Steve Coakley were able to enter the blazing, smoke-filled house to make a search for the victim. They found the unconscious woman on a stairway landing. With the help of 2nd Ass't. Chief Jackie Miller (who removed his facepiece to give the woman air), they got the woman out of the house to the backyard where Chief Miller started C.P.R. until he was relieved by Deer Park firefighter Greg Bianca, a member of Rescue Co. #1, who continued C.P.R. until the woman was revived. She was taken to Good Samaritan Hospital in West Islip by the Martin Luther King Ambulance Corps, where she was treated

Unit of University Hospital at Stony Brook suffering from burns on 40% of her body and lung damage.

Firefighters under the command of 1st Ass't Chief Warren Kompass extinguished the blaze, which was determioned to be not suspicious in origin and was believed to have started by an electric heater.

After the fire was out, firefighter Coakley, who was burned on the neck and Lt. Dunleavy, who collapsed from heat and exhaustion were both transported to Good Samaritan Hospital by the North Lindenhurst F.D. ambulance.

Ass't Chief Miller (At left in photo) looks over the badly burned house.

Text and Photo By
Ernie Ranke, Jr.

127

August 19, '78

July 31, '81, Caught
shark, 140 lb.

April 1979

Dec '89, Tree Trimmer for
Town of Babylon

Steven going to work at
Eng 217, Brooklyn

Steven studying for a test

Heroism award 4/28/87. Steven in uniform next to flag

Steven (in center) at Florida house with members of Engine 217.

Earlier this month, Steve and I boated to Marco Island. It was a beautiful day with flat water and great sunshine. When I went to pick Steve up I said, "You look tired. Do you want to blow this off?" He said, "No way man, I'll get all the sleep I need when I die."

Steve was my friend in the true sense of the word more like a brother than a friend. Now he is my hero. I love him and I miss him. I thought you might want to know.

John Kauziarich, Largo

Carl Francis Asaro

By Sally Asaro,
Carl's sister

Carl F. Asaro was born on October 10, 1961, the third son of Salvatore and Madaline Asaro. He was followed by a set of twins, Paul and Sally, who were born on July 9, 1963. Carl went to St. Mel's Grammar School in Flushing, New York, graduating in 1975. He continued on to Holy Cross High School to be part of the band, playing flute for which he received honors. He was able to play other instruments with ease, a talent which through his life he shared with others. He graduated from Holy Cross in 1979, which made his parents very proud of him. Carl went into the family business after high school. He then took the Fire Department test and passed. I remember when he started working out for the physical. He would go to the local school and run up and down the steps over and over again. There had to be at least twenty steps. I used to pick on him. Now as I think, I wish I could do it—even once would be nice. He graduated in July '87. I took the test a long time ago. Carl dropped me off in my car, which is the only way I knew it was him when I got out because he had gotten himself a "Mohawk" hair cut with 54 and 4 on the sides of his head (those were the numbers of the engine and ladder companies that he was assigned in the FDNY) He always had a sense of humor.

I suppose you could say we were average kids. We had tons of fun. School came first, of course. My mom and dad bought property in the Catskills when they first married, and we spent a lot of time there growing up. There was a working farm there, the owner and my father were very good friends. We would spend weeks there in the summers. We would help around the farm. One summer I was playing with fireworks and blew up my hand and wanted to hide it. Carl and Paul cut off my burnt hair and remaining eyebrows and lashes. I had dinner with my hand in my pocket that night and got caught. I had very severe burns and started school that year and could not write. As you can tell we stuck together. Winters were great, snowmobiling and fooling around with friends. One winter Carl and Paul were riding snowmobiles in a wide open field very fast. They flew over a ditch and Carl's mouth was open. When they landed, Carl had somehow bitten his tongue off. The local doctor was new and was painting a sign on the door. Carl was his first patient. We certainly felt sorry for him.

Dad started to build a house before he passed. He and the boys would all go and work on weekends. Dad and my brothers would go hunting a lot. They all enjoyed the adventures and tall tales. Carl would always come before the season and check his tree stands and other spots. He was always prepared. Opening day

school photo

Paul and Carl

was always a big event. Our Uncle would come hunting every year. The ritual back then was whoever got the buck got to cook the heart. I backed out of dinner on those occasions. We got to hang out a lot and have dinners together. He always waited for me to make him coffee and to serve him. I was always told that Heloiza, his wife, did this for him and therefore why shouldn't I when she was not there? Now those memories have a very special place in my heart.

On September 17, 1982, our brother Anthony was killed by a hit-and-run driver. Carl stood up to the plate. Again, on January 19, 1984, our father passed away. Again, Carl was there. My Mother was the *ROCK* that kept us together, Carl was her *ROCK!*

He always welcomed us at the firehouse. He would drive me home from work when I worked in the city. On a visit from upstate, I was invited to stay for lunch. The alarm rang and the Chief told me to get on the truck, I hesitated and again I was told to get on the truck, so I did. When we got back to the firehouse the

Left to right: Phillip, Matthew, Heloiza, Carl Jr.
Front: Marc and Rebecca

Sally and Carl

Carl's wedding day
Paul, Mom, and Carl

Sally and Carl

Left to right: Anthony, Carl, and Paul

Sally's Memorial Tattoo

Heloiza and Carl Jr.
Carl and Phillip

147th Street, Willets Pt. Blvd.,
Whitestone, NY

Mom and Dad

Paul and Carl
Durham, NY

Carl and family
Rebecca's Communion

Carl, Paul, and family friend
Durham, NY

alarm went off again. This time I was asked to watch the grill so that lunch would not burn. I was always asked to stay at meal time. Carl became quite the cook.

Having two brothers as active firefighters made Mom and me very proud. I was working at Slopes restaurant/bar in the town of Hunter one year after the FDNY ski

Paul Asaro and family

Left to right: Paul, Sally, Mom, Carl, Anthony Asaro

Left to right: Carl, Paul, Anthony, Sally
Whitestone

Carl Graduation, FDNY
Aunt Rose, Uncle Charlie and Carl

Anthony Asaro

"Our little band"
One day just like that at home!, Nov '99
Left to right: Rebecca, Carl Jr., Marc, Phillip, Matthew

races and was approached by a fireman who asked who I knew in Engine 54 because I was wearing an Engine 54 Ladder 4 shirt. I proudly replied, "My brother is the Chauffer." He said, "I don't know about that, but you look just like this guy I work with." He was talking about Paul. I suppose that we do look more alike than I thought.

My brother enjoyed life. Thinking about it, even though his life was way too short, I believe he lived it as he would have liked to. He loved his wife, Helozia. They had a good life and together brought five beautiful children into the world. The twins, Carl Jr. and Phillip, were born June 28th 1988, Matthew August 29th 1989, Rebecca October 24th 1991, and Marc July 24th 1994. All have grown up to be great young adults. I can see Carl in all of them. He definately lives on in his children.

Carl loved his music. He was a great follower of the Grateful Dead. If he had the time he would have traveled everywhere to see them. If there was a game show "Name that 'Dead' Tune in Three Notes" Carl would have won every time. He roped Mom right in; she would sit on the phone to get tickets for Carl. After 9/11 Phil Leash of the band read about Carl's dedication to their band and dedicated the show in NYC that November to Carl. I heard it was a great show. I got to meet Phil at a show in July '02. Carl's close friend Bill Dunigan and I went backstage and got to hang out with Phil. He is a great guy. He autographed a shirt for Mom and again said that Carl really seemed to be very "*Dead*icated." Again, it made me feel very proud.

Carl is a very special person and I don't think that just because he is my brother. I can't end this paragraph without telling about Carl sitting in a tree, taping a Jerry Garcia show in Saratoga while Heloiza was giving birth to the twins. She was early and had no way to reach Carl, so Paul was the man of the hour. Carl and Bill got the message and drove like bats out of hell to get home. Carl Jr. and Phil were there waiting for them, happy and healthy.

How many people can brag about their brother being part of the Stage Actors Guild? Carl appeared in Third Watch, Law & Order SVU, and The Soprano's. He also appeared in such films as The Siege, Frequency, Changing Lanes, and Spider Man. He played a firefighter, paramedic or police officer. Acting was another one of his vast pastimes.

In truth, my mother should be writing this story. She lived long enough to do the things she wanted to. One of the most important was having our street, 147th Street in Whitestone, NY, named "Carl F. Asaro Way." My mother needed to get heart surgery, and afterward she had to be brought back to life. One day she sat me down and told me that something happened to her—she saw Carl and spoke to him. He told her he was there to take her but it was not her time; she still had things to do. He also told her that he was fine and was with our father and brother Anthony. I was immobilized and believed and hung onto every word she said. I have no fear; my mother left me with broad shoulders. My family in heaven is truly missed. My only consolation is that they are together.

September 11th is like yesterday in my mind and most likely always will be. I remember every moment of the day, where I was and what I did. Finding out

Carl was missing, speaking to someone on the hotline at 3:00am, his co-worker at 6:00am. Seeing Paul on TV at 7:00am and feeling a little relief knowing he was safe. Speaking to my mother and Heloiza but no one wanting to tell the other one that they knew Carl was among the missing. I thank God every day that both my brothers were not working. Watching my mother bury two sons in her lifetime was unbearable. I hope that someday Carl and all the other unidentified will be identified. Families deserve that. Our heroes and all who gave their lives on September 11 deserve better.

Jude Safi

By Ahlam Safi,
Jude's mother

To the Present and Future Adolescents of America
From a Mother of a Son Who Lost his Life on 9/11/2001,
World Trade Center

IT'S A BOY

Proud Parents Ahlam and Elias and big brother Johnny Safi
Welcome their bundle of joy into the world

Jude Safi
October 9, 1976
6 lbs-15 oz, 21 inches long

The proud parents, big brother, grandparents, aunts, uncles, and cousins were thrilled with the arrival of baby Jude. Jude was a very pleasant baby, cooing, smiling, and generally capturing the hearts of his whole family. Big brother Johnny was always there for his new little brother, teaching him how to talk and walk and eventually how to play. I, as his mother, and his father, Elias, treasured each moment of our young sons' lives. We brought them up with our morals and values. We taught them the importance of family and friends and celebrated many happy occasions in our home.

As Jude grew from a toddler to a pre-schooler, he wanted to follow in his big brother's footsteps and go to school just like Johnny did. So my husband and I registered Jude in a nursery school, but shortly thereafter he decided nursery school was not for him, and that he would much rather be at home with his mom.

The following year, Jude was a little older and a little wiser and ready to enter kindergarten at Regina Pacis Catholic School in Dyker Heights, Brooklyn. Jude walked into his kindergarten class smiling, easily making his first acquaintances with classmates that eventually became his lifetime friends: Frankie, Pepe, Jason, and Richie, were among them. They had many similar interests, including playing ball and playing chess together, usually in and around the front of our home. In addition, these great friends got into mischief together, laughed together, but mostly enjoyed each other's company. Jude was also known as the class clown and one of the greatest cut-up artists in the school, although no matter what he did, when he turned on the charm, not even his teachers could stay angry at him. One of Jude's very special gifts was the ability to make people laugh and feel happy.

Another story I would like to share involves Jude's First Holy Communion celebration, when Jude put on a show in his John Travolta (ask your parents who he is) white suit and disco—danced for the enthusiastic crowd. He thrived on the attention he received whenever he had an audience, and his confidence was evident as far back as we can remember.

Jude's fourth grade teacher describes him as a happy child with a big smile and beautiful eyes, seemingly enjoying every moment of his life. His eighth grade religion teacher had this to say about him: "Jude was always a respectful young man with a deep desire for knowledge and a yearning for a personal achievement. He also came with a great sense of humor that he often used to put people at ease. Generally, he was a terrific boy who became a wonderful young man."

I recall the time when I received a phone call from the school regarding Jude's behavior in class. The students had to draw profiles of Presidents George Washington and Abraham Lincoln; Jude thought it would be amusing if he had the president's profiles facing each other and sticking out their tongues. Of course, his classmates laughed, but unfortunately for Jude his teacher did not appreciate his creativity—this was just another facet of Jude's sense of humor.

One day while I was putting clean clothes into Jude's closet, I let out a scream due to something scaly and green with big eyes looking at me from a glass aquarium. Jude had secretly concealed his pet iguana knowing that I was not very fond of crawling reptiles.

Abraham Lincoln Feb 1'd   George Washington

Jude and his friends were always swapping baseball caps, polka-dot shirts, parka jackets and other popular items of their time. Once, when Jude and his friend Jason were at Macy's Department Store, the boys were eyeing a pair of platform shoes that happened to be the latest craze. Jason wanted a pair of these

shoes badly and Jude wasted no time in teasing him and telling him how ugly the shoes were. As much as Jason wanted a pair he knew he could never afford them, so the boys left Macy's empty handed. Shortly thereafter, who is the first boy at Regina Pacis to get a pair of the sought after platform shoes? You guessed it, Mr. Big Shot Jude Safi in all his glory showed up at school with the shoes on and everyone loved them. Of course, Jason wanted to kill him, but admitted that if anyone could pull off wearing platform shoes it was Jude and they certainly looked awesome on him.

Jude loved everything about the 1950's bygone era that was before his time, and he really enjoyed the music and style from those days. Jude knew all the lyrics and would think nothing of singing Frank Sinatra or Elvis Presley songs out loud, so much so that one might think he was a fifties rockin'-roller. He also enjoyed the old comedians such as Charlie Chaplin and Abbot and Costello. Jude was a walking dictionary on 20th century cinemas and movie stars.

My son Jude was a true gentleman—always honorable and truly polite. He enjoyed making friends and meeting new people and was comfortable talking to anyone; old or young, rich or poor, Jude could find a topic they had in common. Jude was very disarming and made anyone he met feel at ease. He was also the type of young man who was chivalrous and courteous, opening doors for women and helping the elderly when in need.

I vividly remember on Mother's Day he would not only spoil me, but would always remember his friends' mothers as well and buy them each a single rose. Holidays in general were very special to my son Jude and he was always very generous to family and friends with gifts and kind words.

In addition to his generosity and sense of humor, Jude also had a very serious manner and a strong desire to succeed. For example, Jude needed to achieve a great score on a difficult exam known as "Series 7." Succeeding at this exam was the key to obtaining his dream career of becoming an equities trader at Cantor Fitzgerald in the World Trade Center. Two of his longtime friends, Richie and Rob, already worked at Cantor and Jude, who aced his "Series 7" exam, had finally joined them. The trio were together at last—what more could one ask than to have his dream job with two of his best friends in one of the most beautiful buildings in the world, the Twin Towers, in Manhattan?

Four months later on September 11th, 2001 the evil acts of very evil men snatched Jude and many other mothers' children from this world—young men and women who had everything to live for. Jude's legacy is one of love, tolerance, and acceptance. Jude always aspired to be successful; little did he know that his aspirations would come true. He touched so many so deeply with his kindness, his smile, his intelligence, his caring, and most of all his love for human kind. His greatest wish was to take care of all his beloved, Jude you got that wish! What better way to care for the ones you love than as an angel with God in your corner? Jude, you're in good company now, you have Rob and Richie with you and three young men who met as little boys will now be together throughout eternity.

My son Jude continues to have an impact on the lives of others. From his early school days to his career as a young professional, in the relationships he had with family and friends, his kindness to strangers, his concern for humanity, he still teaches us how to live well. For this reason he will always live on in the thoughts, memories, and prayers of those who knew and loved him.

An annual scholarship fund was established by Jude's friends for Xavarian High School in Brooklyn. "The Jude Safi Scholarship" is awarded to two young men each year that have the outstanding qualities that exemplify the Jude Safi legacy. This scholarship will also keep Jude's memory alive in addition to helping other young men achieve their dreams and aspirations, and in doing so, my son Jude is still helping to make this world a better place.

* * *

My Friend Jude
By
Frank Caagen

This is a little something to let people know what it feels like to have friends. Since we lost Jude, it has been hard to recover. For his wonderful parents, it's been nothing but pain with daily reminders of what it was like. We all love them. Thank you for giving us Jude. For a certain handful of what we call *friends*, the pain runs deep. If you ask anyone of us, we'll all tell you the same, "It's never been the same!"

Back then, all I remember is smiling all the time. Always being happy, and always looking forward to another day with my friend. From retreats to school, to dances or pillow fights in the living room, it was all great times.

Times we will never forget. Sometimes it doesn't feel like it even happened because of how perfect life really was. It's so easy to take things for granted without ever knowing.

Going out has never been the same. Doing anything has never been the same. When I think back at those times—those wonderful times, I realize how blessed we were. We realize how fortunate we were to have a friend like Jude.

I sometimes find myself smiling at the fact that I once knew an angel, because I truly believe Jude was sent here to us to show us how much God really loves us.

Jude was the most loving person I ever met. Always concerned, always there, always smiling, always real. He was true to his words and to his friends who he loved unconditionally.

He once couldn't stand to not see me go to Vegas with everyone for a great friend's bachelor party. Two days before the trip, he handed me a plane ticket with that smile on his face that I'll never forget.

My son now carries your name and through him, I can smile like I used to. I know he will one day have what Jude had as he is being taught by a great friend of a great friend . . .

Michael Mullan

By Theresa Mullan,
Michael's mother

Michael, what do you want to be when you grow up?

Age 5
"Michael, what do you want to be when you grow up?"

"A motorman on the big train".

Age 10
"Michael, what do you want to be when you grow up?"

"A catcher for the New York Yankees like Thurman Munson."

Age 15
"Michael, what do you want to be when you grow up?"

"I want to play the piano like Jerry Lee Lewis and get all the girls."

* * *

Michael spent his grammar school years filled with CYO basketball, bowling, swim team, Boy Scouts, altar boy, and music lessons along with daily games of whiffle ball on Jordan Street and causing mayhem in school that resulted in calls from his teachers.

"Mrs. Mullan, you must come to see me so we can discuss Michael's behavior."

I would very politely reply, "No, thank you. I know Michael's behavior. There is nothing you can tell me that I would disagree with or be surprised by."

It seems Michael had a knack of sending his classmate into gales of laughter and his teacher's hair to turn prematurely grey. After being scolded and privileges

F.F. Michael Mullan, Queens borough
Graduation 1992 AAS Nursing
Patrick, Michael, Theresa Mullan

Theresa, Michael, and Patrick Mullan
St. Patrick Day 3/17/1995

Michael Mullan, 1969

Capt. Michael D. Mullan USAR
Receiving his Captain's bars
2001 Firefighter Ladder 12

Reds Baseball Team
Michael Mullan with sun glasses

F.F. Michael D. Mullan,
going away party
Enlisted in army, 1985

Michael "Happy New Year!"

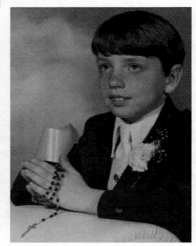

denied, Michael would look at me with his blue eyes and repentant face. "I'll never do it again, Mom. I promise." Well, that would last about a week.

Michael turned in the same Hardy Boys book report three years in a row in 4th, 5th, and 6th grade. In 7th grade, Sister Alban announced, "No Hardy Boys or Nancy Drew book reports will be accepted."

MICHAEL *FINALLY* HAD TO A READ A BOOK!!

Despite all his mischief, Michael had a kind and thoughtful nature. He shoveled snow for elderly neighbors and did errands, always giving a helping hand. He had a paper route to earn his own spending money and always helped his sister with her penny saver route. On rainy days he would do the delivery for her.

Holy Cross High School was 4 years of fun for Michael. I didn't get any disciplinary calls during these years because the Brothers knew how to channel Michael's exuberant energy. He joined many after school activities including the orchestra; the jazz band and the yearly Broadway stage productions.

He was the fiddler in Fiddler on the Roof, Asher in Joseph and the Technicolor Dream Coat, a chorus dancer in Chicago, and Riff in West Side Story, enjoying every minute he was on stage.

At age 16, summer jobs were hard to come by, so Michael signed up for summer duty at a cerebral palsy camp in Rock Hill New York. New campers arrived every two weeks needing total care (feeding, bathing, dressing and exercise). He carried out every task required for the well being of his charge. He finished the summer with much praise from the staff for a job well done. I believe Michael's nursing roots were planted during that summer

After graduation from Holy Cross, Michael joined the Army. "Mom, I've been in school all my life. I need a break."

The Army turned out to be a good fit for Michael. He responded well to the discipline, learned to be focused and set goals. His adventurous spirit earned him a parachute badge for completing three jumps.

Boot Camp finished, Michael returned home on leave. He was eager to see his teachers and show off his uniform. After a pleasant visit and well wishes, Michael said good bye. On his way out, he passed the detention room with 12 sad faced students, heads down, busily writing a torturous assignment. Michael, as mischievous as ever, stepped into the room and with a very authoritative voice said, "Gentlemen, you are dismissed." Instead of the expected laughter and the "Yeah, sure," the 12 students picked up their books, flew past Michael, nearly knocking him over in their rush to the front door.

Michael stood there dumbfounded. "What did I do? I better get out of here quick before the Brothers come back." He, too, ran to the front door.

When Brother Steven returned to an empty classroom, he quickly discovered a man in army uniform dismissed everyone.

NOW after 4 years, I get a call from the principal's office of Holy Cross High School. "Mrs. Mullan, as much as we appreciate seeing our alumni, blah-blah-blah-blah!!" My first though was, "Oh no Michael, what did you do now? How am I going to tell your father? "Suddenly I realized Michael was no longer a Holy Cross student. He was a soldier in the United States Army. He belonged to "Uncle Sam" now. I was finally off the hook. I started to laugh, the principal didn't think the incident was at all funny but I did.

Michael became a legend at Holy Cross.

During the 6 months of his military duty, Michael sat for and passed the New York City firefighters exam. When his 4 years enlistment was up, Michael was honorably discharged with clusters, achievement medals and as a certified X-Ray technician he learned in the support service unit. He followed up by enlisting in the Army Reserves, continuing his commitment to serve his country.

While waiting for his Fire Department list number to be called, Michael attended Queensborough Community College. He earned an associate degree in applied sciences, sat for and passed the New York State Boards and was issued a license to practice as a registered nurse.

Michael was working at St. Johns Hospital emergency room when a letter came telling him to report to Randall's Island to begin his fire fighter training. Because of his military background, he was chosen squad leader. His training was intense and grueling, all geared at teaching every precaution and safety measure to insure survival at the scene of a fire.

After completing training and with graduation over, Michael was assigned to Ladder 12 on 19th Street in New York. Here he had found his second home. He thrived in this house, sharing deep commitment and comraderie with his colleagues and forming lasting friendship.

Michael quickly earned the reputations of being a prankster and teller of silly jokes and stories. Among the many I was told this: The Fire Department, along with the ambulance, responded to all auto accidents. At the scene a car and a Fed-Ex truck collided. The driver of the car was on a stretcher awaiting transport to the hospital, he was very upset and becoming agitated. Michael went over to him to try to ease his anxiety. Looking at Michael he said, "How long do you think they will keep me in the hospital? I have a business to run. I can't stay in the hospital." Michael answered, "Sir, let us assess the situation, you have just been hit by a Fed-Ex truck. YOU WILL ABSOLUTELY, POSITIVELY BE THERE OVER NIGHT!"

Michael's life continued to be filled with music, song, and dance. He loved playing the piano and did a terrific imitation of Jerry Lee Lewis.

Michael was attending Hunter College to attain a Bachelor of Science degree in Nursing. His goal was to become a nurse practitioner. He had also come up the ranks in the Army Reserve and was promoted to Captain.

While on duty one night at Mercy Hospital emergency room, a young boy of 8 years was admitted with a 104° fever. His name was Steven. Michael was assigned to care for Steven and was preparing an I.V. to help hydrate him and bring down the fever. Steven was very sick and very scared, especially of needles.

Michael told Steven if he let him insert the I.V. he would take him to his fire house, dress him in his gear, let him slide down the pole and sit up in the truck. "You can't be a fireman. You're a nurse." Steven said. Michael crossed his heart and told him, "I promise you, Steven, I am both."

Steven let Michael care for him and before long his fever came down and he felt better, making a full recovery. Two weeks later, Steven and his mom went to Michael's fire house and had a great day doing all the things Michael had promised him.

AGE 34   "Michael, what are you now that you are all grown up"

I am a New York City fire fighter.

I am a Registered Nurse.

I am a Captain in the U.S. Army Reserve.

I play the piano like Jerry Lee Lewis and I get all the girls.

"Happy is the man who is rich in good deeds
For he shall be honored and remembered
Long afterwards for his goodness."

Christopher Noble Ingrassia

By Anthony Ingrassia,
Christopher's brother

Chris was always an optimistic person that brought feelings of fun and caring wherever he went. He was blessed by God with outstanding strength, speed, and agility; and he practiced, trained, and developed his gifts and skills to become an outstanding High School and College athlete.

In elementary school, Chris played most all of the organized sports and was great at all of them. In High School, he focused on football, wrestling and track, earning 8 varsity letters. He had the versatility to play almost any position on the football field and was outstanding on the offensive line and as a linebacker on defense. He consistently gave 100% effort. He always kept his head in the game and had great awareness for what was required of him at a given moment.

As a team captain he led by his example displaying great character, discipline, toughness, and loyalty. He recorded what is likely still a record number of tackles in a season his senior year at Watchung Hills Regional High School and was recognized as a great player in New Jersey in many ways. After the football season, Chris went into wrestling mode and proved to be an outstanding heavyweight placing in the State tournament. He had and showed great love and respect for

his fellow teammates, classmates, coaches, and teachers. He graduated in 1991 as the first "Mr. Watchung Hills."

Chris was also blessed with a great mind, and again he worked hard to develop this gift. His achievements in the classroom earned him the invitation to attend Princeton University and he accepted the challenge. He continued to work hard and excelled both on and off the field, then graduated and enjoyed great success in the business world. He was invited to join the team at Cantor Fitzgerald and accepted a new challenge. He worked very hard, traveled throughout the world, and was invited to become a partner in the company. He worked on the 104th floor of the North Tower.

Chris had a great ability to be a ferocious warrior in competition and a great, loving guy when the battle was over. His friends and teammates knew they could count on him to be there for them both on and off the field. It is difficult to summarize all that Chris achieved in sports, school, and his career, but beyond and above the many great accomplishments and awards, it was the life-long friendships that he cherished the most.

Chris's love for sports continued after college as a great Giants and Yankees fan. Even as a fan he was outstanding, with a tremendous ability to recall names, statistics, and situations that he felt were special. When Chris's life on earth was ended in the destruction of the Twin Towers his spirit and memory lived on and continues to thrive in the hearts and minds of his family and friends.

Lessons Learned

Live life to the fullest
Work hard every day
Remember your friends
At work and at play

Be truthful and honest
And loving and kind
Remember your family
Is one of a kind

You're given an opportunity
To start each day new
Don't waste the chance
To thyself be true

Maureen Crethan Santora

Heroes are those who do extraordinary
Things during extraordinary events
May we always remember the wonderful
People who died on September 11, 2001

May we emmulate their traits,
Strengths, joy for living and
Courage

Maureen Crethan Santora

Fire Fighter Michael Dermott Mullan
Engine 3 Ladder 12 Battalion 7
January 16, 1994 - September 11, 2001

1967 - September 11, 2001